WTF
WAS I THINKING
FAMILY BUSINESS

WTF
WAS I THINKING
FAMILY BUSINESS

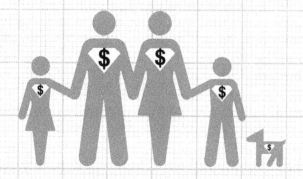

Andy O´Brien

atmosphere press

© 2023 Andy O´Brien

Published by Atmosphere Press

Cover design by Senhor Tocas

No part of this book may be reproduced without permission from the author except in brief quotations and in reviews.

Atmospherepress.com

Dedication

This is a shout out all of you that have inspired, educated, mentored and challenged me to write this book.

First Jodee, Tanner, Kari, Bailey, Austin, Brayden and Ellinor for always believing in me. (Most days). Mom (RIP) and Dad for letting me live to a ripe old age to be able to pen this book along with the work ethic to just get things done. I'm confident from the stories there could have been a breaking point when I was around the age of 5. Ron and Karen for teaching us how to work together in business, even when I thought his name was "asshole."

Brad Sugars, founder and CEO of ActionCOACH, Thank you for an incredible opportunity and allowing me to be part of your amazing company for so long! You continue to pour into myself and so many others every day and I'm eternally grateful to have you in my life.

To all my mentors and coaches, Tom Frank, Curtis, Dennis and John Lewerke, Alain Melendez, Andrew Johnston, Bruce Wilson, Doug Winnie, Dr. Michael Hartley, Monte Wyatt, Don Berry and John Hutmatcher – your teaching, coaching and mentoring is shaping me into the Leader I am today.

Lastly - All of you clients, past, present, and the future- Y'all that continued to push me to write a book based on your learning is amazing. Your trust in me and our team over the last 13 years is an honor!

I'm confident that I missed someone along the way, please note just because you are not written doesn't mean you're not appreciated.

Thank you ~ Andy ~

Contents

Introduction: I was an S.O.B. 3

Chapter 1: All in the Family 8

Chapter 2: Right Sizing Your Business 18

Chapter 3: Give a Man a Fish – Nah – It's time
to be hit with the fish! 32

Chapter 4: The Skinny on the Differences Between
Revenue and Profit 40

Chapter 5: Common Challenges and Obstacles 50

Chapter 6: Hiring is an Art Form 66

Chapter 7: A Primer on Operations 78

Chapter 8: We're All Going to Die One Day: Legacy 85

Chapter 9: It's time to F.I.T.F.O. 93

Introduction
I was an S.O.B

There is something you should know about me. I am an S.O.B. There, I said it. Many of you are now asking yourself, why would he say that? And should I keep reading? Yes, it's safe to do so. In fact, this Son of a Boss has a lot of stories to tell you. But we better start at the beginning. From an early age, all I wanted to do was work with my grandpa and father in the moving business. Every weekend, I would get to go to work with at least one of them and run around the warehouse and play amongst all the moving equipment.

One dream, one goal, that's all I ever had, which was to work in the family business. But dad and grandpa had one rule: if you were old enough to carry something, you were old enough to work. I think this philosophy was ingrained into my father early on, as I have a newspaper article from 1954 when he was working at 14. It talks about the start of Grandpa and how he served in the war and wanted a better life with his wife and kids. How he had become part of a growing industry in Mason City, IA.

There is a memorable story from my early work life. It was a mid-August day in Iowa, and I was working a straightforward local move, stopping to pick up the furniture and move it down the street. But I was in rare form, being lippy to my aunt and dad that I didn't have enough moving help because my partner on the job had to leave early. I was basically a prima-donna, and I wanted to get off early myself, and I saw that

wasn't going to happen at the rate I was going. I became more and more vocal about my situation as the day wore on and I had to do most of the work myself.

Now, where I can be hot-headed and arrogant, my father was the exact opposite of me – he was calm, collected, stern and direct. He said to me quietly, "Andy, if you keep this up, you will continue to work by yourself until you learn to have a little respect for others."

I immediately shut up. My father also always reminded me, "The truck never unloads Itself." It was a great lesson in humility, yet it took me several years to fully understand this lesson and to be able to teach it to others. In fact, it took many such years of learning a multitude of lessons growing up in my family's business, that I now make it my mission to impart to others to help them improve the fortunes of their family-run businesses.

Believe me, there was a time when if you told me that today I would be running a successful coaching business with my own family, and I sit here writing the introduction to my book, I would have suggested you probably smoked something illegal. School was always a struggle for me – I had ADD, ADHD, BSO (that's Bright Shiny Object Syndrome) and about every other combination of letters available to make a traditional academic life difficult and, couple that with a catholic school system where discipline and focus were their mantra, they were going to teach me to listen and sit still. On top of that, I was always the kid who was getting bullied. Middle and high school for me was an endless game of dodgeball run by the school bullies who thought nothing was more hysterical than slamming my head up against the locker, taking turns punching me in the shoulder or a swirly in the toilet. It was hard to concentrate in school, so I always relished the chance to work outside of school whenever I could.

Years later, I look back on the many adventures and experiences that brought me here, and they were often in one family business or another, long after I had moved out into the world to try my hand at working for others other than my own family. So, I learned many ways to successfully and unsuccessfully run a family business.

College didn't work out much better for me. I seemed to be cut out for the world of work, not studying. Luckily, I met my wife on a blind date she was on with a friend of mine (not my fault, by the way!). We hit it off and were married seven months later. She is the person who constantly drives me to be a better man, businessperson, and father. We are blessed today with two kids, two in-laws, and two grandkids. For many years, work discussions became family discussions on Thanksgiving, Christmas and everywhere. Disagreements travel through families – I have five cousins and three sisters. Everyone takes sides. When I was growing up, my dad and my aunt owned the business, and often my mouth got me into several disagreements and discussions with the family at work. Maybe they should have been harder on me, but then again, I think if they had, I wouldn't be where I am today. I now know that those decisions created animosity on all sides of the family; no holiday, birthday family function was safe from the stress in the air.

I am constantly reminded of my early years in the family business as an S.O.B. In 2017, I received a call from Scott, who told me he owned a construction company. He sounded desperate and said he had heard about my coaching services from a friend and asked if I would be willing to help him and his father, Karl, in their business. They were having trouble with cash flow, profit, people, and most of all, each other. I met with them, and we went through my usual intake process. Once we got deeper into our conversation, I started asking questions of them both to get them to tell me their varying answers as to how the company was doing business. Things began to get heated between the two of them. I stopped them and did a verbal DISC assessment (a fancy communication/personality test) of each of them. I gathered data and then asked them each a set of different questions relating to their individual communication styles to determine if there was a foundational crack that needed repairing. After about 30 minutes of DISC education, they each realized that they were not allowing for the differences in their individual preferred communication styles. From there, they were able to start to have more open and honest conversations, which then, in turn, improved their ability to stay in business together. Wow, I could have used this education 20 years earlier in my own relationship with my father.

In the coming pages of this book, you're going to tunnel beneath the hood of what it takes to run your family-owned business successfully. We are going to delve into how to ensure you are the size you need to be for your business to be successful, and not because you feel like you need to hire every third cousin who needs a job. We will look at some common obstacles and solutions to effectively leading your team as well as managing your family members within your team.

We will get down and dirty with the differences in truly understanding revenue and profit, which may reveal what at first may seem like complex, but are more simple solutions to getting this right in your business. You will come to appreciate the very fine art of hiring, which will save you bucketloads of time and stress in the long run. We will do a deep dive into operations so you will fully understand the importance of implementing effective systems and processes, workflow automation, and how understanding the different levels of learning we undergo will help you better understand and manage your teams.

Finally, in the chapter on legacy, you will learn how to not only leave a legacy with your family-owned business, but to set it up so it can run without you, not just because one day we're all going to kick the bucket; but so, you can finally take that damn vacation!

Chapter 1
All in the Family

A family needs to work as a team, supporting each
other's individual aims and aspirations.
—Buzz Aldrin

When I was growing up in the family moving business, there was a saying that my father and grandfather never tired of repeating to me: "Andy, the truck doesn't unload itself!" To him, this was a credo for discipline and focus. I can't even count the number of times I heard this phrase, usually as I was scampering up and down the moving ramp, with other things on my mind than helping move boxes. In my family, you were put to work as soon as you were old enough to carry anything. I mean, anything at all, throw pillows, lampshades, small garbage cans. To say I grew up with an intimate knowledge and direct experience of the dynamics of family-run and owned businesses is perhaps an understatement. It was branded into my cells at an early age. Today, I run my own family business with my wife and son and guide other family business owners and entrepreneurs on how to avoid the pitfalls so common in our entrepreneurial niche, and grow and excel their businesses so that everyone thrives and survives. Literally.

Moving is like a giant Tetris puzzle, and you need critical thinking skills to work out the puzzle; you know, what's the end GOAL? I had an innate ability, or perhaps one learned from a young age, where I could walk in and look at a house and know exactly the size of the moving van needed and how to make it all fit. I have well developed problem-solving and critical thinking skills. These skills, along with the first hand and life-long knowledge of the challenges facing family-run businesses, have enabled me to successfully help business owners improve their companies while maintaining and strengthening their family relationships in the process.

In 1946, my grandfather got out of World War II and bought a little delivery service company they named Snyder Delivery in Mason City, Iowa. My grandmother worked side by side with my grandfather in the business. By 1954, it had become O'Brien Moving and Storage, and my grandpa started buying more trucks. They had bought a big semi-truck and a franchise license with National Van Lines and continued to grow. My father went off to join the military, but when he got out, he returned and joined the family business. Mom never joined the business, and they met in 1967. By this time, the business had grown big enough to house its headquarters in a six-story warehouse. They would take the trailers that come in on the railroad, which was called piggy backing, unload them and drive them to the locations and vice versa. It was a big transfer, storage and moving business back then. Then tragedy struck: in December 1969, the warehouse burned to the ground.

It didn't slow them down for long. They found another spot and moved into a new warehouse, and the family business continued as it had been to usher in the third generation – me and my cousins. If I wasn't in school or sports, I went along with my dad on most moving jobs. You were helping out, or you were running up and down the ramp, trying not to get yelled at to stay out of the way. Sure enough, when my son was old enough to do the same, it was exactly what he did. Growing up in the moving business, all I ever wanted was to be a part of it and do it better.

I also grew up with ADD and ADHD, so it would probably surprise no one that my talents lay in places other than academics. When the teachers would complain to my parents that I couldn't sit still and so wanted to punish me by making me stay inside for recess, my parents suggested they have me run around the school a few times to get me to settle down. My parents clearly knew more about how I ticked than the teachers did. Did they take my parents' advice? Of course not. So I slogged through school and somehow managed to survive the slings and arrows of an education system that was never set up to cater to what we now have a name for – neurodiverse brains. Nor did the other kids have any patience for my differences. Being small and definitely un-athletic, I was more often than not the target of endless bullying and the favorite bullseye of the jocks and juvenile delinquents.

But, dear reader, luckily for you, I survived, and my years of hands-on experience growing up in a multi-generational family business have made me uniquely prepared to help other family-owned businesses navigate the most common traps of doing business with your kin.

In this chapter, I will unpack some of the most common issues that families contend with when you have husbands, wives, parents, children, and other relatives all working in the same business together. The rest of the book will take you through the paces on how to figure out what is the right size for your particular business, thoughts around leadership, finally understanding the difference between revenue and profit, the many layers of hiring, everything you need to know on operations, the down and dirty on sales and marketing, creating a legacy, and some parting advice. Fasten your seatbelt; it's going to be a fun ride!

Converting Adversarial to Alliance

Sometimes we get caught up in our silos of knowledge and experience. A "that's the way we've always done it" mentality. For example, I am 54 years old, and I have 35 years of experience in my field – first, the moving business, then sales, and then coaching family businesses. It's easy for me to feel superior in my knowledge around someone with less experience, who might happen to be my 32-year-old son, Tanner, who is our Financial and Marketing Officer. A few years ago, he said to me, "Dad, you don't think big enough." It brought me up short and took me back to a moment when I was trying to help my dad, my uncle, and other relatives bring new assets into the business. I remember telling them we could do this and that, we could grow and we could put storage buildings up and I was met with a wall from them: "No, that's competition. We don't want to deal with that."

I had value to add to this conversation. I don't know if I'd been in the business two or three years with them when this really started to happen. But that feeling of being shut down sticks with you over time. Eventually, I had to step away from the family business to find out that I could indeed do things on my own, but more on that later. Sadly, what I often see happen is that the kids in the family business are either ignored or taken for granted.

When the tables were turned on me, and my son made that suggestion, I admit my first impulse was to get mad and shut it down. But instead, I decided to take a breath, listen, take it on board and see where it took us. We need to know when to recognize that our other family members in the business may have fresh insights that we just have never thought about before. In the case of my son, taking his advice has proven to be the best thing I ever did. Since Tanner joined, we have quadrupled the business, added four new employees, and guided hundreds of owners just like you.

Even if that hadn't been the case, the perspective of a son or daughter with a new idea, or even an opinion, needs to be validated because they might see things that we've never seen, either because we've been in the business too long to recognize it or our offspring might just have a new idea. I definitely saw things that my dad had never been able to see, and my son carried on this tradition for me.

When you give someone the space to hear them out, and to be open to conversation around the idea, then you validate them and avoid unnecessary conflict. Let's face it, every idea that any of us has is not going to be great – but by doing this instead of shutting them down, we keep the lines of communication and respect open, which is one of the most fundamental aspects to maintaining good business partnerships within the family unit. Be open to a dialogue on the issue or idea at hand and back it up with facts, rather than emotion. Because when emotion gets involved is when it always gets dicey.

Creating Boundaries

One of the most consistent and recurring problems I see within family businesses is the lack of boundaries. Christmas, Thanksgiving, Easter – every holiday dinner is a board meeting. Things that should be left for discussion in the workplace get dragged home to the dining room table, and vice versa; personal issues come out in the office where they really shouldn't. These issues, along with others, can lead tempers to flare and fester over time. Often, during my process of working with a family business, I have to advise a husband, wife, parent and a son or daughter to go take five and cool off, before coming back and resuming the Coaching conversation.

Especially when the entire family is in the business. For example, my grandfather died in 1981, just after he had retired at the age of 64. When he retired, he never told my dad where anything was nor gave him any information on the financial life of the business. As you can imagine, it was a hot mess and took months to untangle and decipher. Don't do this to your family. Once my grandfather died, my aunt and uncle joined the business full time, so then we were really all in the family – all in.

Think of creating boundaries within your business, like using a mesh grid or curtain in front of your fireplace. The sparks will still fly, but they are less likely to catch the house on fire or land on your kid's head. The first thing you can do is draw up what you could call your manifesto, rules of the game, or just a list of what is unacceptable and what is acceptable. This document needs to be clear and available to everyone to read, ideally created with everyone's input. It should be a living document, and by that I mean one that evolves and is updated over time as both the business and family members grow and change.

One of the things I highly recommend you have in your manifesto is a list of things or topics that stay at home, and those that you can discuss at work. Don't bring your personal issues into the workplace. It's not only bad for your team's productivity, but also downright awkward for other employees. Plus, it should go without saying, it's really bad for your family relationships, which are exactly the ones you need to preserve to keep everything running smoothly?

By the same token, don't bring your workplace issues home. An example of this is that I am very good with numbers and budgets at work. But who does the books at home? My wife, Jodee, and she won't let me anywhere near personal finances. And no, she is not a control freak. I just happen to suck at them when it comes to our own finances. My wife is a former CEO of United Way of Williamson County and North Central Iowa, an international non-profit, so believe me, this is the right way all around. She also joined our family business as our CEO in February 2022. So now we are all in with walking our talk and learning as we go.

Also, while we all have a version of short-hand language

we use with family members, be wary about talking to them in ways that differ hugely from your other employees. Reign in your critical judgment faculties, and when you do need to give feedback, filter it through a language test by asking yourself how you would give the same feedback to a non-family member employee.

A few other things to keep in mind that will keep better boundaries with family members both at home and at work:

- Don't give them decision-making power that is not warranted by their position in the company. For example, if they are in a more junior position, they don't get carte blanche to design their office like an Ikea showroom unless that happens to be your company policy.
- Don't give them higher status locations or job perks than their status warrants.
- Distribute your family members throughout the office, if not remote working, so they are integrated with other employees.

Husbands and Wives, Brothers and Sisters

A special note on these relationships within the family-owned business. Sometimes, the roles of husbands and wives can delineate along cultural stereotypes when it comes to roles at work and home. But this needn't be the case. Do what works for you and best suits your working styles and relationship. Basically, what I'm saying is screw stereotypes. The most important thing is that your business runs well and your home life runs well – not what other people think about how you achieve that! Give each other the freedom to work in whatever role suits each of you the best.

There can also be troubling dynamics between siblings,

especially if one kid is favored in the family as being more responsible, organized, or efficient. Just as with partners, siblings know how to push each other's buttons like nobody's business. According to a recent Forbes article on just this topic, "Setting boundaries around separation of duties becomes even more important when siblings have significant differences in their approaches to problem solving."[1]

Staying in Your Lane

There could be nothing truer said than everybody has an opinion in a family-run business. I know; you're already groaning and nodding your head in agreement. As the saying also goes, there is no "i" in team. Staying in your lane refers to when family members try to get another family member on their side behind an issue within the business. For example, if you work in manufacturing, stay in manufacturing, don't weigh in on how you think things should be done in the sales department. When everyone has an opinion about everything, usually coupled with emotion, it can quickly become a raging brush fire.

Family-owned and operated businesses don't have a clear organizational chart for the seven pillars of business: CEO, Finance, IT, HR, Sales, Marketing, and Operations. There is no clear line of sight because there are three names in each area based on need in that moment. To create clear lanes, there needs to be ONE person/owner of each area, and that person is responsible for that area, with daily, weekly and monthly KPIs that are tied to the company's yearly OKRs. Yes, and even family members can be fired for not fulfilling their roles.

And don't let passion get confused with emotion. They are two different things, and they can get erroneously coupled together and used as a default mechanism to weight an issue towards a desired outcome. "Mom, I'm just passionate about the business. Don't you want me to be passionate?"

"Yes, but now you're being emotional. The data clearly

supports the fact that we need to do a, b, and c." You can see what this conversation might look like. Let's look at traditional businesses – offices like the CEO, IT, marketing, sales, operations, finance and human resources, and we will get into organizational charts later. In most family businesses, there are multiple people doing the same jobs, like sales and marketing. So let's put two of your kids who are passionate and competitive with each other in these roles, and instead of running as one unit, you now have created two silos.

"That will never happen at my company," is the typical line. I am going to call B.S. on this. When you raise kids to be competitive, in school, in sports, for example, your kids will win at all costs, and that means a human sacrifice of another family member or another employee to help them look good.

I have been guilty of this often enough myself and have been known to let my emotions get the best of me. My dad and I had a major disagreement one day, and it killed me to quit, but I had to. His name was on the building; mine wasn't. I had no money or risk, and he had it all. I had not yet gone out into the world to work in any other business but ours, and it really was time for me to spread my wings and see what I could accomplish on my own. As it turns out, I found I was very good at selling.

I started by selling office supplies. This was a necessary step for me to go out on my own, and it is a recommendation I make to many of my clients. Some of them already require their offspring to go and work elsewhere before coming into the family business. There is validity in this approach and many upsides. The least of which is the value gained in learning the ropes of a work environment without the shackles and emotional ties to family dynamics. It is useful for them to learn to be wrong as well as take orders, suggestions and opinions from others.

Years later, I realized my dad was completely right in the argument we had that I chose to quit the business over. But sometimes, when you're too close to it, you can't see it. And in my case, it was time to leave for a while.

Some other basic things to keep in mind when trying to establish good boundaries in your business: in the workplace, address other family members by their names, not by 'mom' or 'dad' or whatever familiar nickname they may go by or term of endearment you may have for them on the home front. Also, try to use more open-ended language to invite brainstorming sessions, such as "tell me more about your idea," rather than shutting people down too quickly just because you've already decided it's not up for discussion or a good idea. You might be surprised where a more open-ended approach will lead you. As a parent, we believe we need to be right and if you think your age requires someone to respect where you have been. YOU are WRONG! I'm not saying you won't be right sometimes, but if you have these limiting beliefs, you will kill your family based on your ego, not your logic.

In the next chapter, we will explore what it means to 'right size' your business and how, just because someone is a family member doesn't mean they should be working for you.

> Action Item #1 – If you're struggling with any of these issues in your business, here is a gift that keeps giving! Email us at andy@andyobrien.biz to get your complimentary questionnaire to show you where you need guidance and collaboration in your business.

 Key Takeaways

- ➢ Work to separate business and family;
- ➢ Find ways to create boundaries;
- ➢ Define clear and concise roles; and
- ➢ Know when to walk away – just because they're family, are they a good fit for the organization?

Chapter 2
Right Sizing Your Business

Coming together is the beginning. Keeping together is progress. Working together is success.
—Henry Ford

One of the biggest challenges I see family-owned and run businesses facing is the concept of what I call "right sizing your business." Too often family members will be put to work in the business simply because they need a job. "Cousin Bobby is looking for work and wants to help out." What is Cousin Bobby's skill set? What is his work ethic? Does he play well with others? Too often these questions are left unanswered, and Cousin Bobby is put to work in sales when, in fact, Bobby couldn't sell his way out of a brown paper bag.

Right sizing your business also means not just avoiding hiring family members who would be better suited to helping you carve the turkey at Thanksgiving, than increasing your revenue, but it also means having the right number of employees in your business. Just because your first cousin Larry says, "Do you need somebody to sweep? My son Donny can help out!" Hire based on what the business needs, not what you'd like to do for people. Where are the holes that need plugging?

A lot of times with family businesses, we have people doing things that don't bring value or profit to the business. The cold, hard truth is sometimes you must look at family and acknowledge that they're just not a good fit. That's a difficult conversation to have, but sometimes you must be willing to say, "I'm sorry, but you can't work here."

Some companies put rules in place that sons and daughters can't come into the business until after two or three years of working out in the real world for a boss who isn't a family member and who's going to tell them what to do. This is a good example of putting controls in place to ensure that the right family members are working in the business and they are not being assigned to roles just because they are family.

Right sizing your business also applies to the solopreneur who is so used to doing everything herself that she can't begin to think about delegating so she can grow and expand her business. By now you have probably encountered the term, "Work smarter, not harder." Yes, I'm talking to you, dear solopreneur – chief cook and bottle washer of your own empire – if you want a thriving business, which doesn't mean being the next McDonald's or Best Buy, it will behoove you to pay close attention to the suggestions in this chapter so you can save your sanity while running a profitable business and not killing yourself in the process.

But first, I want to tell you a story of a family business gone horribly wrong that I once worked for. I had been working for a high-end wood cabinet company doing sales. I traveled up and down the Midwestern corridor for several years, and I learned a lot of great lessons working for this company. They were a family of jokesters who pranked their employees and each other constantly. They'd put pennies or salt in your coffee, put holes in your water bottle. They thought it was all hysterical, and they thrived on shenanigans. How work ever got done I'm not sure, but it did. I think they managed to create such an easy going and convivial atmosphere that people loved working with them, and so they worked hard. However, because the guys who ran this company were constantly pranking people, they would even go so far as to have fake people call you and try to lure you away from the company with another job offer. They thought this was a good way to take the temperature of your loyalty. However, I also knew that it wasn't likely to be a company that I could move up in because it was completely family-owned and run. The owners had sons and daughters in all the key roles in the company, which was about to teach me a lot more than I already thought I knew about nepotism.

One day, I got a call from someone who said he was the CEO of Woodport Doors and Flooring, a huge competitor of theirs. Of course, I absolutely had no doubt that this was one of my bosses pranking me, so I said something rude and hung up on him. Not long after that call, I received a call from a headhunter who said, "Andy, what the hell did you do? I heard you hung up on the CEO of Woodport!"

I felt my blood run cold. "What do you mean?" I asked.

"Yeah, you idiot, the CEO just called to talk to you about a job – I told him to. You better fix this." And the line went dead as he hung up on me. So, I had to call the CEO back and eat humble pie. I was lucky he gave me another chance after I explained about how my current bosses would often prank us. I eventually did get to interview for that job and, after a long process, he hired me.

It was just after the 2008 crash and ensuing recession, and while I had enjoyed and done well as an independent consultant, I was keen for a bit of stability that the job as a national sales manager would offer with Woodport. Nevertheless, things went well in the beginning, and I went from national sales manager of a $60 million dollar business to Senior vice president within a short period of time.

What I didn't know at the time I started at the company was that it was in the middle of a private buyout that was going on behind the scenes. However, one day, as I was driving to the factory in Shawano, Wisconsin, I got a call from the original owner of Woodport Doors, who was at the factory, which was odd because he wasn't usually there. By the time I got there, he had taken back control of the company and had removed the CFO and the CEO, who were both in the buyout, and he had brought his friend in to be CFO. And so that began my lesson in shitty management and ownership and all the wrong stuff to do. Effectively, he derailed the buyout and tanked the company.

Over the course of the next year, the owner took an angel investment from the State of Wisconsin and deposited it into a private account. Early December 2010 was the first chance I had to see the financials of the company. I noticed a line item with self-insurance that the owner had not paid in 90 days. Our son and daughter were both athletes. Tanner was a college swimmer and Bailey was swimming in high school at the time, so I called my wife, who, as I mentioned earlier, handles all the home finances and said, "You need to get insurance for us now." The company had not paid the insurance premiums and was hemorrhaging money.

If you learn anything from this book, I don't tell my wife what to do unless it's an emergency.

This drama ended with the Assistant Attorney General of Wisconsin, along with a Deputy Sheriff and a lot of suits, walking into the company and escorting the owner and his co-conspirator, one of his trusted allies, out of the building, as those of us left sat there, shell-shocked at what had just transpired. The five of us in the top management were assured we were going to get paid; we were the lucky ones. The State of Wisconsin came in under a 127A, which they enforce when a business is insolvent. They took over the company a few days before Christmas, and I got to fire 164 employees that day. Over the next several months, a consulting company was hired to come in and dismantle the company and sell off the assets, and I had to do my part to help ensure vendors were paid.

In total, they owed vendors about $21 million. After the only assets, two buildings, were taken back by the lender, $9 million was still owed to vendors, eventually tanking several of the vendors.

I tell every business owner, regardless of size and scope, you need two As and two Bs. What this means is you need an accountant, an attorney, a business coach, and a banker to right size your business. Because the cliché that it takes a village to raise a child is not wrong, it takes a village of your trusted advisers to successfully run your business. Similar to the idea of outsourcing what you least like to do or are the least good at, admit to yourself that you may never have the skills to be the CPA of your business, nor do you want to be. Focus on and figure out what you do best, and let the other experts take over the stuff that you don't do best.

Family-run business owners come to me, at the end of the day, because they want to solve their top three challenges. They desperately need more time, need to hire or train trusted employees, and want to increase their profits. I tell them this will be an apprenticeship for them. They will study business processes and learn how to do them all the better than they have been. Because whether they are an ophthalmologist, an oral surgeon, or they sell wood siding, the processes are all going to be very similar, and the tools they need to hone them are surprisingly universal. But when the rubber meets the road, I often hear, "Oh, we've been doing it this way for 35 years," I nod, smile, and respond, "Well, we're going to change that." I also ask them to look at their cell phones. Is it the same as it was two years ago or even ten? It used to be we would talk about change as the 70s, 80s or 90s – now we discuss change in 18 months or shorter time frames.

Raising prices and Maximizing Margins

Raising prices is an area that usually scares most people to death. Why? They fear they will lose clients. But when we start to talk to business owners about raising prices, we use our system that shows leads to conversion rates to clients. We discuss average dollar sales and the number of transactions, which leads you to revenue, and then we discuss maximizing margins and pricing. Think of it like this: if I had a gun to your head, and I said to you, dear reader, "Have you thought about raising your prices?"

You adamantly and vehemently shake your head no and say, "I'm not going to do it!"

But if I say, "I can calculate by raising your price that you'll get $5,000, $50,000 or even $5 million more."

I go on, in my best understanding tone, "I know how scary that is for you. Let me ask you, do you have $5,000 in the bank you can give me right now?"

"No, of course not," you say.

"OK, then tell me, why would you give your customers $5,000?" I respond.

You insist you're not doing this.

But then I show you that indeed you are – by not raising your prices. Because we run a mathematical equation that shows you that if you're not going to do what's best for your business, you might as well take that $5,000 you have in the bank, go out to the parking lot and set it on fire. Because this is the equivalent of what ends up happening, people don't correlate a price increase with a loss of profit.

Perhaps this hasn't made enough of an impression on you yet. I want you to stop and consider your expenses over the course of a year, such as insurance, rent, utilities, fuel, and more. You may not feel these expenses until the end of the year when you suddenly are hit with the "Oh my God, I don't have any money left!" moment. Now you begin to understand the raising your prices equation a bit better.

Your profit margins are what is left over after you have paid all your expenses in the business, including yourself. I've worked with businesses that are turning over $1 million who, at the end of the day, are only making a 1% profit. That's $10,000 out of $1 million. Not ideal, right?

The first priority is to grow your margins. This is the number one way to help your business grow. Too many business owners are always looking to cut expenses, but the truth is no business can cut its way to long-term success. If this was on a bumper sticker, it would say, "Jumping over dollars to pick up pennies." We can cut today and help the bottom line for this month, but eventually, to grow, you must increase the number of clients, and you must increase transactions and average dollar sales. We look for ways to increase them across the board.

Think of it this way. How many times do you go to the barber or hairdresser during the course of the year? If you answer three to four times, your hairdresser is leaving money on the table. Because their job is to schedule you to come in every three to four weeks, instead of a quarter, before you leave the salon. We have worked with (and this applies to) hairdressers, massage therapists, chiropractors, fitness facilities or any service business. When you're considering raising a price, if we put you in every three weeks, you will get 13 transactions a year in your business. Because there are four months that have five weeks, the mathematical equation is to do your billing on a weekly basis because you get an extra month of billing per year per client. Then, when you start doing the math, it exponentially changes the profit numbers.

Example of a fitness facility we have worked with for many years: 2021 price per month is $92 a month. 300 members ($92 × 12mth × 300mbr = $331,200 per year). Pretty decent year for most who want to own a job.

Suppose the 2021 model was weekly: $92 / 4 × 52 = $1196 per year x 300 members =$358,800. This would have been a $27,600 increase in year one if they weren't afraid of losing members.

2023 model: $92 x 26% increase = 115.92 / 4 × 52 = $1506.96 pyr × 352 mbrs = $530,449.92.

Another common theme with family-owned businesses is that owners run a lot of their personal expenses through the business. We informally call this a "checkbook business." Maybe you'll buy a new boat or use some money from the business for a down payment on a house, or maybe you'll go and buy a jet ski, trailers, bigger tires, and rims. This is going to come back to bite you, trust me. To maximize your margins, you need to pick out those things that can be reduced in the business and moved to the personal side of the business. Sometimes it may be about consolidating notes and debts for maximizing margins, or maybe you need to renegotiate your lease. Or maybe you need to implement minimum charge policies.

Whatever it takes, you need to start tightening up your terms of trade. Whether it be not paying overtime, switching around work schedules, there may be any number of possibilities. Because at the end of the day, it all adds up. Once, we worked with a very large cement mixing company that did an analysis and found that when their mixers were driving down the road with their tumblers spinning all the same time when empty, this put extra stress on the motor, which in turn used more fuel. This was after they had dumped the concrete, and they didn't bother to turn off the tumblers. Once they noticed this, they made this adjustment, and the company was able to save $1 million in fuel costs in one year. They also looked at when and where their drivers stopped to refuel. They would often drive out of their way, maybe only by five miles, to find cheaper fuel and get their favorite snacks at their favorite truck stop. This was also examined and changed to a set route they were not allowed to veer from. We helped them install fleet management software that tracked this and created huge savings for the company.

Your business will improve exponentially when you start examining outcomes and key results for the year, then further back that into quarterly or 90-day periods, then back that into a monthly plan, and then further back to daily planning that is reviewed and examined at these points.

Definitions:

OKR – *stands for Objectives and Key Results. It's a collaborative goal-setting framework for companies, teams, and individuals to set challenging, ambitious goals with measurable key results. Monthly, Quarterly, Yearly.*

KPI – *Key Performance Indicator (Per person – Daily, Weekly and Monthly).*

KAI – *Key Activity Indicator (Per person – Hourly, Daily).*

KBI – *Key Behavioral Indicator (Per person – Always).*

In this process, you will create KPIs, KAIs and KBIs that you will live by and each of your staff is required to do. These should be considered the "Minimum Standards Required to work in This Business." This needs to be non-negotiable. Further to that, if you implement, monitor, and adhere to these KPI's, KAI's and KBI's, you forfeit the right to complain about your family and employees. It's a pet peeve of mine that I often hear business owners complain about their employees, whether they are family or not. I repeat: you hired them – you forfeit the right to complain about them.

Working on the Business

Learn how to work on the business instead of in it. I cannot take credit for this phrase, as it has become a well-known maxim in business. But you would be surprised how many people still fail to grasp the concept. So, let's break it down here: the difference between the two comes down to working on the day to day operations of the business and working on the big picture that helps your business grow and operate more effectively. For example, fiduciary responsibility or managing your finances once a month or, as some need, once a WEEK – otherwise known as planning! This includes working backwards from your five-year planning, three-year planning, one-year, 90 days, and monthly. Set your goals for each of these periods. Notice they are time bound. This is incredibly important. Parkinson's Law is an oft-used adage that states, "work expands so as to fill the time available for its completion."[2]

Too often, we spend our days being reactive. Everything is a fire that needs to be put out now, if not yesterday. I know this is hard, but I want to encourage you to carve out blocks of time (15, 30, 45, 60 minutes) in your calendar, even if it's only two hours to start with, where you can be proactive and focus solely on this critical aspect of your business. That is why putting processes and systems in place is so critical. That is why delegating and outsourcing, either what you don't do best or hate to do, is so critical. In David Jenyns' book Systemology, he walks entrepreneurs through the steps to relieve the overwhelm and create a finely oiled machine that works independently of its specific parts. "When your business becomes a collection of interdependent systems that can be engineered to deliver extraordinary outcomes...you are no longer dependent on specific team members for things to work. The systems work, and the people work the systems. This is a different level of business, where you're able to rise above the noise and be deliberate and strategic in the work you do. You can begin to optimize your performance."[3]

Chunking time or setting aside a block of time where you work *on* the business rather than *in* it, can allow you to work out ongoing problems that don't get addressed in the day to day putting out fires mode. For example, say you run a retail clothing store, and you want to make sure that the inventory you're buying from manufacturers is turning over right away. Because, if you put ten grand out today, your product doesn't come in for 30 days, and it takes you another 15 days to sell it. Now you have a 45-day cash gap where your output is greater than your input. You must manage all of those things, and you can't do it if you're *in* the business every day dealing with customers or putting out fires, which are sometimes one and the same thing.

Play to Your Strengths, Hire to Your Weaknesses

This means exactly what it sounds like. If your sister, Sue, is working in the business and she is great at sales, don't put her in accounting. If your son, Darren, is very techy and prefers interacting with screens rather than people, don't put him on the sales floor; get him to work in IT. I'll use myself as an example. I am very organized in my work world and can work well and advise on anyone else's finances. When it comes to the family finances, I humbly and happily pass the baton to my wife, Jodee, as I said in the last chapter. Know your weaknesses and play to your strengths – it will serve you well in the long run. When I realized that my strengths are coaching and inspiring people, it allowed me to let go of things I thought I should be doing, but frankly wasn't that good at, like the operational aspects of the business. Hence, my son Tanner joined the business in 2020 and now runs our operations.

It also bears repeating, don't let yourself get caught up in gender role stereotypes of who should be doing what. If you can let go of outdated ideas based on gender or family roles and where they should be in your business, you are putting the best interests of the success of your operation first. Once you stop looking at your business as "this is the way we've always done it," you will be setting the stage for excelling.

The Rules of the Game

For those of us who speak freely and it was put on a "Bumper Sticker," all the shit that has pissed you off over the years from your employees and family not being trained correctly is considered a rule of the game. The rules of the game mean setting up the minimum standards required for your business you are not prepared to compromise on. I like to call this the Right to Work for Our Organization. I used to use the word expectations, but I concluded that sounded too much like a disciplinary word. Standards are more inclusive because they apply to everyone within the enterprise. The way you figure out what your minimum standards are is to work backwards from your desired outcomes. What is each person responsible for, and what are their outcomes each day? Each week? Each month? Each year? From there, you back that into their minimum standards and responsibilities for each time period.

When we set up minimum standards for work performance and behavior within the company, that then gets rid of things like nepotism or other instances of people being treated differently because they are family members. Things become much more straightforward. I call it the "right to work for our organization." Of course, we didn't have anything like this in place in the family business I grew up in because we were not that sophisticated at the time. But I have found that now, when I coach businesses through this process, it quells infighting considerably, and it helps people stay in their lanes and focus on their own role and not others.

One thing that falls under this category I call Staying in Your Lane. This is an area that is violated daily in family businesses. This keeps infighting to a minimum. For example, someone working in operations tries to tell the salespeople what to do. Then salespeople tell IT how they think things should be done. You get the picture. Be responsible for your own outcomes and don't try to steer the whole ship. This often gets muddy because, as discussed in the previous chapter, people have not created good boundaries between personal and family interactions and those appropriate for the workplace. My message here is unequivocal: stay in your lane and be responsible for your own outcomes, not other people's.

ORGANIZATIONAL STRUCTURE

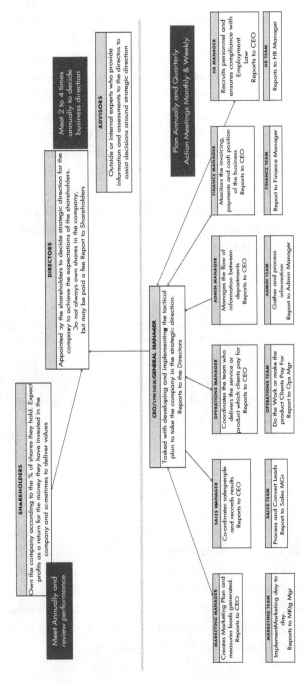

Action Item #2 – You want to know if your family is in alignment in the business? Email us at andy@andyobrien.biz for your Expert complimentary strategy alignment session.

 Key Takeaways

- Don't be reactive in business; always look for solutions;
- Picking your partners and proper buy-sell agreements save time, energy and a shit ton of money;
- Don't hire your friends;
- Don't try to screw the government at the expense of your people;
- Raising your price is an emotional fear, not a reality;
- Figure out where you can maximize your profitability;
- Understand the difference between working *on* or *in* the business – set up systems; and
- Play to your strengths, hire to your weaknesses.

Chapter 3
Give a Man a Fish - Nah - It's time to be hit with the fish!

Give a man a fish and you feed him for a day; teach a man to fish and he'll buy a funny hat. Talk to a hungry man about fish, and you're a consultant.
—Unknown

There's a proverb that you've probably heard by now: Give a man a fish, he'll eat for a day. Teach a man to fish, and he'll eat for a lifetime. I have my own addendum to this saying, which is, "Sometimes you just need to hit him/her with the fish." Let me explain. One day, I was having a conversation with one of my mentors, Tom. This was at a point in my life when I was traveling full-time. I would spend one week a month at the factory, then three weeks a month on the road. Every time I got to the factory; I'd never get out of the door until at least 10 o'clock at night. Because, all day long, I had this revolving door of meetings with people, I wouldn't be able to get any actual work done until the evenings after most people had left the office.

I was running myself ragged, felt like I was burning the candle at both ends and wasn't performing optimally. I wanted to talk with Tom about this, so I managed to get a meeting scheduled with him. I was so looking forward to it because I just knew he would have some nuggets of wisdom and experience for me. So, I showed up for my highly anticipated meeting with him and explained my situation, and all he said to me literally was, "Oh, that's interesting. When you get it figured out, let me know." Disappointed, I left his office and reviewed our meeting in my head. Was there some hidden advice somewhere I was supposed to read between the lines? Did I miss something? I reviewed my notes and couldn't find anything. I waited what I thought was an appropriate amount of time and tried again – made another appointment with his assistant and went back in.

This time I told him, "I'm psychotic. I'm losing my mind with busyness, and I can't get things done." All he said to me was, "So, how did you get in here?"

"I called Julie and got on your schedule."

"Isn't that interesting?" he said.

"Is it?" I answered, totally confused at this point.

"Well, when you figure things out, let me know."

So another month goes by and I go back in. Same story all over again. Only this time, I said to him, "Look, I don't understand what your point is. I am totally perplexed."

"It's simple," he said. "Put up a schedule. Don't let people interrupt your time. When people want to talk to you, they say it will only take a minute. But that turns into 30 minutes before you know it."

The light bulb went on over my head. I said, "I get it now. You just hit me with the damn fish!"

Sometimes, we all need to be hit with the fish. Think of it as helping you see the light at the end of the tunnel and to have situational awareness. This means learning how to take yourself out of the situation, and also removing the emotion from the situation so you can see it and your role in it more clearly.

> You must be a good follower before you can be a good leader.
>
> —Unknown quote that i love

We've all been cultured by good and bad leadership in our lives. We can usually vividly recall both the best bosses and the worst bosses we've ever had. We also intrinsically understand that people naturally have different leadership styles. I appreciate the military approach to leadership, that it is a skill that can be trained. Nevertheless, I do believe that leadership can be broken down into different areas, and we all naturally gravitate towards one type or another. For example, there is Positional Leadership, which is the lowest level of leadership, there is Permission Leadership, which is when someone grants you permission to lead. There is Productivity and Results-based Leadership. Then there are what I like to call People Growth Areas, and finally, there is the Top of the Diamond Leadership.[4]

Positional leadership is when somebody is assigned a leadership role based on their position in the family. For example, I recently had an executive leadership conversation where there were the owners and a general manager, and the son was away at college. The general manager wanted to know where does the son fit in? Was he going to be replaced by him at some point? This is a natural way for employees to think. Am I expendable? We had to discuss putting people in positions based on their experience and not their role in the family. If the son is a better technician, maybe that should be his position in the company, not one of leadership. Because if they decided to make him a manager, then he would become one over his peers who may have potentially been better qualified and earned it. When you don't pay heed to these dynamics, you will end up with resentment among your ranks. Are you kidding me? How did he get the job? Why didn't I get the job?

Avoid positional leadership like the plague.

With Permission Leadership, the person has earned the right to lead because of something they've done and the trust that they've developed within the organization's people. The hardest thing about this area is that people can get stuck there and forget that they're there to help bring people up with them. As a leader in the family, are they helping others grow? Are they helping others succeed? Are they helping them reach their goals and hit their KPIs? Or do they walk into a meeting and say, "Oh, look what I did?"

Because when that is the prevalent behavior, the message that is communicated to other team members and employees is that they only care about themselves. The best leaders know how to motivate their people to GSD – get shit done! And getting shit done is what productivity and results-based leadership is all about. On this level, leaders who produce results build their influence and credibility. People still follow because they want to, but they do it because of more than the relationship. People follow these leaders because of their track records.

The Productivity level is where leaders can become change agents. Work gets done, morale improves, profits go up, turnover goes down, and goals are achieved. The more you produce, the more you're able to tackle tough problems and face thorny issues. Leading and influencing others becomes fun, because when everyone is moving forward together, the team rises to another level of effectiveness.

Then there are people growth areas, which is about how leaders in an organization help bring others up with them and develop them into higher positions within the company. I remember once when I was working as an independent consultant rep, and I got hired by a family-run business; I knew that I would never get into a higher management role or accept a leadership role within that company because every leadership role, except for the Chief Financial Officer, was a family member. When the kids grew up, they became the National

Sales Manager, or the Vice President of Sales, or the Head of Customer Service. They just funneled their family into all the higher positions, so I knew I would never go anywhere with them. It is not uncommon to see a lot of nepotism in family-run businesses. My family was guilty of it too. I remember thinking I was hot shit as could be, and now, when I look back, I realize I was nothing more than a glorified truck driver. At the end of the day, I was loading furniture. People thought I was the son, so I could do whatever I wanted to do in the company. For a time, I admit I thought that too. But then I always got in trouble, so I learned my lessons in entitlement early.

Finally, at the top is Diamond Leadership. I believe that all good leaders float between that place where they're developing others and they're being selfless in helping other areas of the business. There are only a few people who fall into that Diamond or Pinnacle area, like the Brad Sugars', Marshall Goldsmiths, John Maxwells, Bud Grants, Phil Jacksons, Tom Landrys, Bill Belichicks, or Kirk Ferentz's of the world. They have put so much out into the universe that they bring the same back in.

When we discuss leadership, we're essentially talking about how to be a trusted adviser. And there is a process that we go through with every client, which is about building trust. People hire a (or firm of) executive, business or leadership coach(es) because they want more time, they want a better life, and they want more money. They're looking for guidance, collaboration, and they're looking for somebody who can help them get to the next level. This trust period must be worked on with every client, and that goes for any family business as the same thing that needs to happen between family members, as it does with employees. If your employee does something wrong, they're held to a different standard in most cases that I have seen with fathers and sons and mothers and daughters. Likewise, vice versa, the family member is always held to a different, harsher standard. I've seen the nepotism, but it's usually because they're trying to swing the pendulum so far in the other direction. And this is where things get murky. Is it leadership, or is it punishment?

When I find myself going down this line of discussion with a business owner, I often stop the conversation here because otherwise, it leads to emotional outbursts. When the conversation gets emotional, I ask them a simple question, "What does this have to do with the business today?"

This can happen a lot with husbands and wives who work together, and it does not lead down a good rabbit hole. Oftentimes, the thread of the conversation will lead to subject matters that have nothing to do with the business, which is where things get murky and relates to my earlier discussion about boundaries in family businesses. When we are focusing on leadership, the goal is to change behavior, change perspective, or sometimes both.

I ask them, "What if another employee did this? And it wasn't your wife? Or your son or your daughter? Would you talk to them the same way?"

I often hear back, "Well, they should know better."

"Why should they?" I ask. There is often a double standard when it comes to family members, and this is a familiar refrain I am often urging my clients to open their eyes to. Because when we talk about leadership, one of the greatest compliments we ever get is when we start hearing our clients mimic our language. I help business owners to understand that part of effective leadership is to sometimes find a better way to handle the situations that often come up with their family members and employees. They learn to ask themselves, "Could I have handled it differently?"

Family business owners have often made the mistake of thinking a family member would never quit the business. Then I'm there to remind you that I quit my own family business as a young man. But we always leave judgment out of it because it is not constructive. I suggest that you ask your employees more open-ended questions like, "So tell me, what got in the way of you being able to be calm? Or dealing with that situation differently?"

Maybe your son or daughter will respond, "Well, I was pissed off." I would then say, "Great, are you mad at them, me, the situation, or yourself?" This question interrupts their thought pattern and encourages them to focus on the root cause and not their emotional reaction to the event.

You can say, "Yes, I got that. But what was the barrier to doing things a different way? If you remove the emotion from the equation, we can find out what was stopping you." This is a simple redirect of what got in the way of A, B, or C. This takes it out of the realm of personal attack or judgment, which you really want to avoid at all costs. It's about getting to the root cause, not just focusing on the symptom or laying blame.

The truth is, every parent and business owner have, at one time or another, had trouble separating their personal relationships from the business relationships and environment. We're all only human, and it's a slippery slope for most people. But good leadership is about behaving with empathy. It's about saying, when something goes wrong, "Look, I know where you're coming from, and I've been in your shoes before." Or, "Let's table this for a minute and unpack it so we can see what the issues really are." Because good leaders ask great questions. They don't assign blame, judge, shame or give a guilt trip. Good leaders learn to navigate those muddy waters with their family members. And discipline is private, not public. Because when it's public, especially in a family business, then it becomes humiliation.

Business owners don't really get a business apprenticeship in school. Most programs teach the skills of the trade they happen to be in, but they don't teach people how to run their own businesses. One of my first ever clients in our business was a dentist, and he and his wife were co-owners of their practice. His wife told me one day, "You know, some days we're just lucky if we can agree what side of the bed we sleep on." Then the husband admitted, "I went to college to be a dentist. All I want to do is drill in fill all day long. That's my role. They didn't teach us business courses then."

They were good at being dentists, and they had a successful practice, but they weren't as good at running their practice. And they really wanted a more successful practice so they could sell it. In order to do that, their business apprenticeship consisted of getting them out of the business. I had to get them out of doing payroll, or worrying about health insurance, or all the various areas they needed to be delegating to others. So that when somebody wanted to buy it, the value of the business would go up exponentially by 40% if it was running smoothly. The more and more we get business owners out of the day-to-day business, the more successful their businesses will become.

There is a happy ending to this story. After about two years, they were able to get the price they wanted for the practice and were able to exit the business and start new ventures.

> **Action Item #3** – Do you want to learn more about yourself and your management and leadership abilities? Take a 360 assessment and learn what others in your business think about you. Email <u>andy@andyobrien.biz</u> for your assessment.

 Key Takeaways

- ➤ You must be a great follower first; then and only then can you lead;
- ➤ Teach first, then HIT them with the fish; Hire Coaching, FFS to figure it out;
- ➤ Understand that not one of you is as smart as all your people combined; and
- ➤ Keep your personal shit out of the business.

Chapter 4
The Skinny on the Differences Between Revenue and Profit

Remind people that profit is the difference between revenue and expense. This makes you look smart.
—Scott Adams

When we talk about revenue and profit, we all know that is the end-result in all businesses. People can always tell me three things about their business: how many clients they have, how much revenue they have in business, and if they made any profit. But they don't always understand the difference between these last two things. Because if I say, "That's great, Dan, what are you going to do for next year? How are you going to do it?" I'm often met with blank stares.

"Well, I want to grow my business by 20%," Dan stammers.

"OK, great. Tell me what that means to you?" I say.

And he tells me, and we do the numbers. "So, if your business is bringing in $200,000 and you say you want to grow your business by 20%, that will be $240,000 business next year."

Dan nods.

"Oh wow, that's great," I say. "How are you going to get there?"

"Well, what do you mean?"

"Well, how are you going to get there? How are you going to measure it? What are you going to do for it?"

"Umm..." Dan scratches his head and looks off to the left, hoping he might find the answer lurking in the corner of the room.

If I'm not getting anywhere by then, I say, "Let's back up. Tell me how you came to that number? Is that number from revenue or profit?"

"Yeah, that's from revenue." Dan brightens.

"Ah, that's what I thought. Here's the problem with that," I say.

Then, I go on to explain that we need to look at a lot of other areas. We need to look at the other seven areas in the business: MQL (marketing qualified leads); SQL (sales qualified leads); true leads or opportunities; conversion rates; number of transactions; average dollar sale; and margin dollars. Now let's look at your MQL (marketing) – how many people are you touching through digital, social, networking, ads or talking to on the street? Are they a marketing qualified lead (MQL)? Are they raising their hands and asking you for more information? If so, we can write/put a number down.

From here, we can look at if any of them are SQLs. Do they come voluntarily?

MQL
Probabilty %
=
SQL
Take Up %
=
Opportunity
Conversion %
=
Clients
X
Transactions
X
Average $
=
Revenue
X
Margin
=
Profit (Gross)
Money Net Profit

Do they want an opportunity to buy our products? Now we have traction.

Then, let's look at your conversion rate (sales). This means that for every four people you talk to, if you enroll or sell one, that's 25%. Then we move onto the Number of Transactions (customer service) – how many times do they buy from you every year, month, week or day?

Now we look at your average dollar sales; what else could they buy from us today? And it goes back to that conversation in the last chapter about raising your prices. Now we have that pesky revenue number that doesn't change unless we measure and add to the above equation.

Now let's talk about the most important area – percentage of profit margins. As I've said before, and I will say it again, if you're not working to make a profit, you should just go get a JOB (Just over Broke). Everyone can save a few pennies here and there, but you need to build profit into every area of your business, including your time, so they tie together.

This is when we start looking at revenue and profit in the business – it's great to look at the revenue, and nine out of ten times, we will beat their numbers when they start focusing on the other areas of the business rather than the end result. For example: if you have a million dollar business that does a million dollars in revenue, and you spend $999,999, then you're just turning dollars. Every dollar out means you're not making anything to go with that. And that's what we must look at. The profitability number at the end of the P&L and balance sheet are the critical drivers in the business (and coach to the balance sheet because that's your equity/money). Many family business owners today want to employ family members; they want to bring more people in, and they stop looking at profitability. "Cousin Donnie needs a job. Let's hook him up." OK, there goes 40 grand right there.

When I ask them what value Donnie is bringing to the business, I often get vague answers.

"Well, you know, he's helping out here."

This is where we need to set family on one side and business on the other and say, "OK, I understand, you are a person – you're a father, a son, a mother, a daughter, you are an uncle, an aunt and you are also the business entity over here, and we have to set ourselves up as a business that allows family members to come in, when they're qualified, when they're skilled, and when we need them." Because one thing I always hear is, "You know, we just don't have any balance. We don't have any time off. Our team sucks."

As I have said previously, I have zero tolerance for business owners who complain about their employees, whether they are family or not. When you hire them, you forfeit the right to bitch and moan about them.

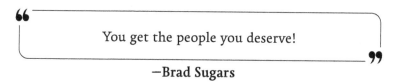

> You get the people you deserve!
>
> —Brad Sugars

I work with you, the owner, to help you start to look at your business as an entity, like a living, breathing organism. How much profit does your entity need to make to sustain life for you? Of course, we don't just want to sustain life; we want you to flourish. So, how much money does your business entity need to make to move it forward and bring in a profit? Those are the questions you need to take a long, hard look at and answer.

Action Item #4 – Go back to the chart and add your numbers into the equation. Which of the numbers do you actually track today? Call me today for your seven-ways yearly spreadsheet download.

The Catastrophic Killer

A million dollars in revenue and a million dollars in expenses is what I call the catastrophic killer. For example, a lot of business owners don't feel that they have trusted advisors – that they can trust the bank, their accountant, etc. But in truth, they'll go to the bank, they'll get some advice, and they won't follow it. Then they'll go to their accountant, they'll get the same advice, and they won't follow it. What happened during the pandemic was a prime example. So many business owners were turning dollars – they had revenue, but they also had a ton of expenses. Their revenue dropped, but their expenses didn't. Fast forward to when the loans from the government came out to offer support, and many of you did not have relationships with your bankers. As I've said previously, our philosophy with every one of our clients is that they still need their two As and two Bs – to that end, you must show your banker your financials.

People say to me, "That's not their damn business!"

"It was none of their damn business until you knocked on their door and you needed cash," I reply, as kindly as I can. Our principle behind that is if you had a banker, that you had a relationship and open communication with someone who saw your financials every quarter and had a year's worth of financials, or 18 months. Then, when something like a global pandemic hits, and you approach your bank, now the bank has all of this documentation to look at your history and say, "Oh, my gosh, these guys are running a really good business."

They could go to their lending committees and their board and say, "You know what, this is a good business. It's viable. They have assets, they have consistent revenue. We can do a line of credit, or we could loan money against inventory or against assets." They could do a lot of things, and now you have options.

When they went to the bank, they were able to get that

extra line of credit or be protected before the government helped people out. Now the other people who never went to the bank beforehand to develop a relationship, maybe they were late with their bills, maybe they weren't, but when they went to a banker who didn't know anything about their business with, "Oh my god, here's my financials. I'm really in dire straits. I need money next week to make payroll!"

Well, now the banker's hands are tied. And they look at their business model and say, "Oh, my God, you've got a million dollars in revenue, but you've got a million dollars in expenses. Hey, Dan, I need you to cut; you must lay people off. You're going to have to make massive cuts." You know what happens next? Family business owners who haven't dotted their i's and crossed their t's lose their minds.

"Freaking bank, what do they know?! They're stupid!" Dan yells.

No relationships, no options. Simple as that.

This is where I once again assume my most even-keeled voice and remind Dan, "Well, it's not their fault. They have compliance. They have to follow rules." This is an extreme example because nobody saw Covid-19 coming. But if you back up to 2008, nobody saw the sub-prime mortgage crash coming either. And all of the regulations were put in after Freddie Mae, Fannie Mac, and all of them failed, were restructured, and/or sold off.

We must use our business as a tool to help our lives grow, not vice versa. That's what I mean by catastrophic killers, because at any given time, if you're just turning dollars, then your bank at some point will look at that and your debt to income ratio, and it's going to be so bad, they're going to cut you off. They're going to ask for payments on assets, and they're going to ask for another person to co-sign on the loan. There are so many other ways to look at your business. That's what bankers will do. And they've done it repeatedly.

"Oh, hey, I'm sorry you are over-leveraged. Hey, do you have

a house or a car? Anything that you can put up against this?"
"Well, no."
Then you're in trouble. Don't let this happen.

> **Action Item #5 – What is your debt-to-credit ratio?**
> Current assets/Current liabilities = The amount of liquid assets available to liquidate current debt to the company's ability to meet current obligations.

Your Tools

One thing I've learned over the years is that most family business owners don't budget. I suggest running a six-week minimum to six-month maximum cash flow analysis. Then you need a 12-month budget. Will this be easy? No, it won't. I'm not going to lie to you. It takes most operators about two years to master budgeting and reporting, and it will save your business's life, trust me. And once you get it in place, then you will know your numbers. You will have a running tally of what your expenses are. A good example to work with is companies that have a lot of equipment and are running high fuel costs. Since fuel costs have jumped 60-70% In the last year, having a budget you can measure against, even when you use last year's numbers, will help give you a clearer picture of your projections. Maybe raising your prices to cover the cost of fuel or even a fuel surcharge is reasonable.

Now you know this line item is going to go up, so you must budget for it. You can't project that you're going to have $20,000 in fuel costs then make $20,000 worth of cuts to cover it. It doesn't work like that. What revenue goes to that? The first thing is building a budget. The second thing is how does that bring you cash flow? As you look at a budget, you can tie it together. You can start plugging in actual numbers; you can start projecting cash flow in the business over the next six weeks and six months. It works itself out. And as you do that, that helps you manage the business from a numbers aspect. (Business is MATH and people.) Because cash is king. Interest rates are going up. We saw it in 2008, and we saw it again in 2020. Those businesses that had good cash flow and had money stockpiled away struggled just like everybody else, but at the end of the day, they were better positioned to be able to move their business forward long term. Those who don't have any savings and don't have any profit built into their business are going to feel the pain. Across the country, we saw millions of bankruptcies in the face of the latest unexpected crisis to hit us.

Action Item # 6 Run a quick cash flow analysis.

Knowing Your Margins

You can manage your margins hourly, daily or weekly, but as a business owner, if you're not doing a P&L and balance sheet till three or four weeks (this is a lagging indicator) into the next month, it doesn't help you to manage today. By building budgets and break-even calculators, it can tell us what we need to sell each day. I want you to ask yourself, "What does it cost to run my business every day?" If you don't know your break-even today. You will not be able to answer several questions that are coming up in the following chapters.

There's some guerrilla math that you can do. You could take your overall expenses from last year and you could divide that by 52 weeks. And then you could divide that by five days, and you could come up with a number for what it costs to open your business every day. And that's the break-even calculator. Let's say, for instance, you do all this math, and it comes down to $5,000 (cost) being break-even to open your doors every day. We know some businesses are going to sell

$25,000 one day, they're going to sell $4,000 the next day, but at the end of the week it should all equal out. The idea behind the break-even part of it is to make sure that you know how much it costs to open your doors every day. That is a critical driver because you need to work backwards to help you know what your costs are. Because if you don't, it's hard to know how much you're supposed to sell and how much revenue you need to bring in to get you to the profit you, your business and your team need in order to open tomorrow.

Leaving money on the table means pricing your products based on what somebody else is selling for rather than the value of the product itself and your business. Business owners fall into the trap of comparing themselves to a giant like Walmart. "Walmart is selling it like this!" Who gives a shit? You are not Walmart... You don't have the buying power and cash to compete against them.

And I say, "Well, yeah, if I bought 74,000 containers from some other country and put them on a shelf, I could sell it for a lot less too!"

You need to look at what your true target market is. Then you must base your prices on the value perceived.

My work as a coach is measured based on results. We don't want to leave money on the table based on our value. We can't put ourselves up against Target, Walmart, McDonald's, or other major chains. People always think that everything should cost the same. My mother-in-law always says, "Well, so and so's going to charge me this and so and so charges double that. I want to use him, but he should lower his price to hers." There are different caveats. Prices are based on overheads, insurance, payroll, bricks and mortar costs and any number of things. Maybe Bobby down the street, who's running a business out of his pickup truck, doesn't have any bills, so he should be able to charge less. It's about leaving money on the table. We're trying to compete with people who aren't at our level of competency. **Most business owners grow to the level of their incompetence.** So remember, the world values you based on the value you place on yourself.

> Action Item #7 – Want to create a budget based on the next three months? Email us at <u>andy@andyobrien.biz</u> for the free download of your yearly budget.

 Key Takeaways

- ➢ Know your numbers;
- ➢ If you don't measure your numbers, you can't fix, adapt or grow them;
- ➢ If you don't learn, learn, learn about profit, you will not have any; and
- ➢ Profit must be built into all aspects of your business, including your time.

Chapter 5
Common Challenges and Obstacles

Success is due to our stretching to the challenges of life.
Failure comes from when we shrink from them.
—John Maxwell

There are many common challenges and obstacles that rear their heads repeatedly in family-owned businesses. As discussed earlier, boundaries are one that never seems to go away. Someone brings a spouse into the business, marital problems develop as they are working together, then suddenly, marital problems become problems at work. Or maybe it works the other way – work problems get taken home and played out there. Neither is good for the successful running of the business.

If this sounds familiar, ask yourself: "What does this problem you're arguing about have to do with the business today?"

This question usually gets people to stop bickering and realize the futility of going down that road.

I have gotten many sheepish looks from people when I have posed this question time and again, at which point I will remind them, "If it doesn't have anything to do with the business today, you need to leave that stuff at home." Now don't get me wrong, I understand that marital problems can be a serious wedge in the business, but it doesn't belong in the workplace. Because then everything will go sideways and pear-shaped. Or it might be a mistake that a son or daughter makes or made when they were younger. Again, if it doesn't have anything to do with the business today – forget about it! So, if you are a parent in this situation, I encourage you to have some compassion and empathy for mistakes you undoubtedly made when you were the same age yourself. "Jesus, God, the Messiah or your deity have dropped the charges; why won't you, your son, daughter, aunt, uncle, etc?"

I am happy to be a prime example of this. I was all of 18 or 19 and working for my dad, we were moving an orthodontist from one building to another. My cousin Scott and I decided, to save time, we would throw the cushions from the first story down to the lower level, catching them, of course. Boy, did we get into trouble with my dad and Uncle Joe. Fast forward 25 years later, I'm hired by the same orthodontist office, same office manager, and the first thing that came out of the Office Manager's mouth was, "I remember you and what you did as a kid." We are not defined by mistakes at that age, even if they may be memorable. Luckily, she forgave me.

Language matters and I still suck at it some days.

Instead of using family names like Mom and Dad, or any other nicknames used at home for kids and siblings, try to use people's actual names in the workplace. I understand it might seem odd at first, but trust me; you will get used to it. It is a layer of professionalism that you can add to your family workplace relations that will start to have an effect once you become accustomed to it. In my own family workplace, my son, Tanner, calls both my wife and me by our first names.

When we use language that is inclusive and free from family relationship assignations, it can also make communication easier. It gives space to be able to say, "Tell me more about your idea," rather than just shutting down a suggestion from a son or daughter. Youth might not possess the wisdom of age, but they are often able to look at things in new and innovative ways that we have lost sight of. I also believe that the true test of being able to understand something inside out is the ability to explain it to a kindergartner.

> **Action Item #8** – If you are the owner, CEO, president, etc., SPEAK LAST and not until everyone has expressed their ideas, strategies, tactics or opinions.

Encouraging dialogue and brainstorming sessions, as well as allowing people to speak freely without shutting down the conversation, can both bring about new ideas and improve communication and trust. At the end of the day, assholes are like opinions – everyone has one. They are never in short supply. And there is a lot of posturing for position within the dynamics of a family-run business. Make the space for these conversations (in the office), and you will reap the benefits.

When we first brought my son Tanner into the business, I used to joke that you learn from your past, but you must lean into the future. What I mean by this is that part of our identity is tied to every decision that we've ever made. So, when Tanner came into our business, he had all these new ideas. And he had equally as many challenges to bring to decisions that I had made. At first, I would take those personally and get pissed off about it. Then my own coach (yes, we all have coaches) got me to see that I was living my identity in my past decisions, but it wasn't about who I was as a person or my abilities. Tanner had some fresh ideas on how to do things. The fact is, they were good ones, and I had to be willing to see things through a different lens. This is hard as a parent, a sibling or any other relative because we get attached to our past decisions and our ego of being wrong. If you're willing to walk into a new space and look and listen differently, it can be good for everyone involved – including the business.

Since having that BFO (Blinding Flashes Obvious) moment myself, it's made it easier for me to help other business owners – and parents – have that moment for themselves. It's an important moment to have because, as in our case, bringing Tanner into the business increased our revenue and productivity tenfold.

Paying Debt Down Too Fast vs. Not at All

Baby Boomers and Gen-Xers both believe debt is a four-letter word they want nothing to do with at all costs, and if they accrue debt, they will throw money at it to pay it down as fast as possible. While this may seem noble, it is not always the best method if it leaves you with no cash reserves for dealing with unexpected or emergency situations.

The reason for paying down debt over a set period/amount of time is so you can monitor it for exactly these reasons. Too often, I've seen people get caught in a tight spot when they've had a bad month and no cash flow, and they are suddenly hit with a major capital expenditure like needing a new piece of equipment. This is where cash flow forecasts are imperative for your enterprise, as well as a margin built in for the unexpected. This happens a lot in seasonal industries like, for example, construction, where work often dries up in the winter months due to frozen ground or other severe weather conditions. You want to make sure there is enough money in the bank to get through these periods.

One method is to consolidate some of your debts into one loan. This may lower your interest rates as well. You may have a longer re-payment plan – five years instead of four – but now you've freed up $5,000 a month that you can keep in your cash reserves for emergency situations. Or perhaps this cash flow will enable you to hire another employee so you can delegate some work and further systemize your business. The point is now you have options, whereas if you throw all your cash at your debt in one go, you may end up right back where you started, or worse, in even more debt than you were to begin with. This stunts more business growth as much as not having any sales.

Building a Relationship with Your Accountants

We have worked with several accounting firms over the last decade to help them with their family-run businesses. They are no different than you; in fact, they are like the cliché, the cobbler and his wooden shoes, "Everyone's kid has shoes except the cobbler's family." As I have said before, you need two As and two Bs. Let's talk about the other A – your accountant. I've heard so many times, "I can't afford to pay an accountant!"

My response is always, "You can't afford not to pay for your CPA. They're your 'Save your butt button' in your business."

Today's IRS government regulations are a 75,000-page manifesto on their ability to take your money. Now, don't get me wrong, this isn't an anti-government rant; this is a fact. Accountants are there to provide you and your business with the "peace of mind" that all your business and personal assets are protected and to help you and your business to keep as much profit as you can without going to jail. They are there to provide you with oversight into your daily, weekly, monthly and yearly bookkeeping and provide you with a fresh set of books by the second week of the next month. Having your books cleaned up, running on cash or accrual is essential to being able to measure against your budget.

A rule of thumb: "If you're not testing and measuring your financials, you cannot manage them, and you cannot improve them."

Budgets vs. actuals is a great lesson in patience and insight. People often ask me why this is. I understand that, at first, a 12-month budget might seem like a harrowing task. But I promise you, the first time you build a monthly and yearly budget, it will open your eyes to gaps in your business. (Your accountant will help you put all the bills into the correct category.) The first rule is to see what you haven't been paying attention to and start testing and measuring it. Maybe you don't want to know, or maybe you don't know how to read your financials, but by having a good accountant, they will be good at explaining what your financials say about your business.

Two great questions to ask any CPA:

- When do you reconcile your books?
- When do you file your taxes? (Do you ask for extensions!)

Action Item #9 – Call your accountant and take them to lunch. Ask them all the questions you're afraid to ask or afraid of the answer to! The only dumb questions in business today are the ones you don't ask.

Sometimes, we are all sprinkled with a little "Dumb dumb dust"!

There is an expression called "jumping over dollars to pick up pennies." What this means is that when people start looking at their business expenses, they get solely focused on, for example, the salary of what it costs to hire somebody. "Oh, my God, that's $40,000 a year." And they get stuck in the "Oh, my God, that's $40,000 a year; we can't afford that" scarcity mindset. We are constantly talking them off the ledge because it's not $40,000. At the end of the year, yes, it's absolutely $40,000. But it's right now that matters. We discussed earlier the equation where rather than hire somebody for $20 or $18 an hour, they'd rather do that themselves. And if it's a million dollar business, your hours as the business owner equate to $500 an hour (1,000,000 / 2000 hrs = $500). What they forget to do is the math equation on the $40,000 salary. They

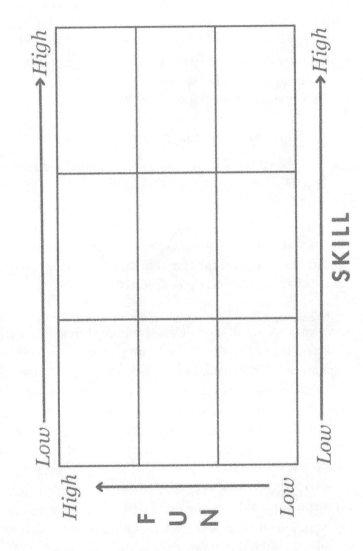

REVENUE

$ _____ /2000 = _____

Highest Paid		Lowest Paid

Role _____   Role _____   Role _____
Role _____   Role _____   Role _____
Role _____   Role _____   Role _____

Duties _____   Duties _____
_____   _____
_____   _____

Hourly Rate _____   Hourly Rate _____

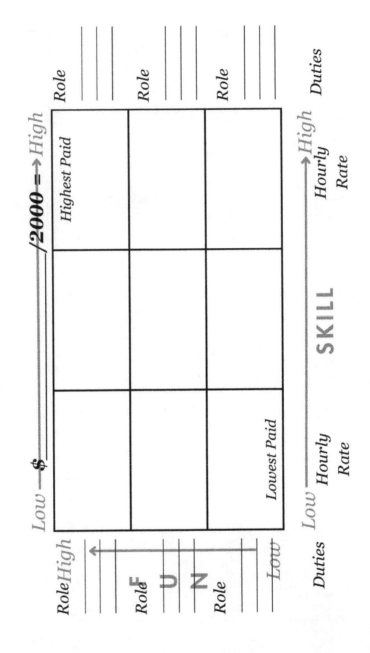

just see the whole and say, "I can't afford it." Rather than breaking it down to $20 an hour, times 40, which is $600 a week, which is $2,400 a month. Your job is only to figure out how to make that $2,400 a month, not the entire 40k. Every employee we hire must have a 30-day review; by 60 days, they should be paying for 80% of their standards and at 90 days, they must be hitting 100% of all their standards in order to keep their jobs. "Period." What they do is they'll jump over the dollar and pick up the penny and say, "Well, one of our existing employees can just pick up the slack."

What they don't look at is if their time is valued at $500 an hour and it gives them three extra hours in the business, that's $60 in expense and $1,500 in productivity. At the end of the day, it's a simple math equation that most people don't take the time to do. Once they do, they look at me sideways and say, "Are you serious?" I love these lightbulb moments.

I do this equation daily for people. I use our business as a litmus test because when we started putting people in positions that played to their strengths and hiring better people, we saw the law of procession at work. Our business got better and better and grew and grew. It's these simple yet incremental changes, **1% every day**, that will make a world of difference to your business. This also goes back to the same idea of being over-invested in your past decisions. Well, this is the way we've always done it. Or I can do it faster than anyone else, so I might as well do it. We think we must do everything. It's like back in the day when we had to convince my father to first get an answering machine (remember those things?), and then after he bought it, he still had to have someone answer the phone all day long. We said, "Dad, that's what the answering machine is for!"

"No, no, someone has to answer the phone," he would say.

You must be willing to start looking at everything objectively and breaking down the math.

> Action Item #10 – Figure out what your time is worth to the business based on a 40-hour work week and two weeks vacation. For all of you saying I work more than that all the time... Maybe you're part of the problem.

Incremental Growth

Incremental growth simply means planning for smart growth over time. It's so interesting that we talked to so many people, and they always can tell me, "Oh, I'm at $100,000 or $1,000,000. I want to have a 10x growth."

"Great," I say. "Well, how are we going to get there?"

"I don't know," they usually respond. "We're just going to do a million."

"So let me get this straight – you're at $100,000, and you want to be at $1 million by the end of the year?"

"That's right."

"OK, great. Who do you need to become to be able to run a $1 million operation?"

This is usually where they look at me blankly and say, "What?"

Because here's the thing. We must start with different thinking, different education, different ways of looking at everything. This is usually the hardest shift. I've lived it. I've seen other business owners that live it; they cannot shift from the now to the what if. I grant you this is a massive thinking shift, but it's one that must happen. For example, our goal is to be a $100 million firm. Now, there have been times when my son, Tanner, has told me, more than once, that I think too small. He has helped me with my ability to think bigger and expand my mindset. Before we can ever get to this point of being a 1, 10 or 100 million dollar firm, we need to develop a totally different mindset. You can't get caught up in the day to day. You can't just do the same stuff repeatedly every day. The first step is working backwards from your end game plan to figure out how you're going to get there. What is the definition of insanity? Doing the same task over and over, expecting a different result!

Let's say you run a bakery, you've been open only a year. You'll need to sell a lot of loaves of bread at $5 a loaf to get to those million dollars in the first year. But let's map out getting to $200,000 to start with and use mathematical equations to break it down. How much reoccurring revenue do you have to have for a $200,000 business? And what do you need to sell? Who's your target market (fogging a mirror and having a heartbeat is not a market!)? And what's your average dollar sale? Once you have your numbers, then you're able to work to those numbers. We get your team to start buying into the vision so they can see where you want to go. Then you implement systems and processes to handle your influx of customers and free up your time to work *on* the business rather than *in* it all the time. We will cover this more a bit later in the chapter.

> **Action Item #11** – What is your average dollar sale? Yes, all of your sales divided by the total tickets. Invoices or customer count.

What is your 90-day plan? Surviving is not the correct answer!

To achieve business mastery, the foundation of your business may need to be repaired. It is imperative to always look and see where you want to head. Yes, a plan is your road map to success. In today's world, you don't just leave home and expect to get to (you pick the place you've never been) without your phone and GPS. This is how you get to your three, five, and ten-year goals; and then work backwards from there. Create your budget and forecast for growth based on where you want to see yourself. But remember to budget for the unexpected, like that new $1000 piece of equipment that you didn't know you were going to need.

Many family business owners suffer from super-hero-itis. Come on, admit it, you really believe, down deep, that nobody can run it better than you. Nobody can do it faster than you. You might as well do it yourself, so it will just get done. Right? Well, I'm here to tell you that is the dumbest thinking in the history of the world. I can say this because I've done it myself. It short-changes the business and stunts its growth, while also not giving your other team and family members the opportunity to grow and shine.

Marketing Too Much vs. Not Enough

If I asked you to give me $5000 from your bank account, would you? For nothing, just because I wanted it. Would you? No measuring, no ROI, just $5,000. Would you do it? Most of you who are reading this do this with your marketing dollars. You give away $5,000, and then you don't measure it or get a return on investment.

People seem to think that marketing is throwing a lot of crap out online or putting up advertisements in any medium, and it doesn't matter if the ads are poorly written or if they're written by somebody who has nothing invested in the process. This is marketing that is too much, without thought, and at the end of the day, for nothing. It asks for nothing, it exists for the sake of itself, and there is no call to action. I encourage you to boil marketing down to some simple factors. I call it WIIFM – or What's In It For Me – or rather, your customer. When you're writing your marketing piece in any medium, whether it's an email, if it's a text message, radio, Digital, Web-based or TV, etc., think about what's in it for them. Not me or what I think it should say because I own the product or service. Your message can't be the same for a 40-year-old as it is for a 60- or 20-year-old. You must change the message for each demographic. STOP thinking you're the judge of your product or service and making marketing about your feelings.

Instead of putting your face on a billboard, web, digital, social or print, think about what you want to communicate and get your viewer, reader, or listener to do. Because the fact is the only person who really wants to see your face on that billboard is you and your mother. No one else, trust me. So when you spend money on marketing, make sure you know what your ROI, or your return on investment, will be and how you will measure it. Without that, you might as well take your money out into the parking lot and set it on fire. Because everything you do, you should be able to measure it with your acquisition cost. Now listen carefully; there are plenty of other steps between the numbers. You'll have to call us for the MQL (marketing qualified Lead), MQP (marketing qualified presentation), and SQL (sales qualified lead). For example, how much is it if you spend $300 on any type of marketing for two weeks and you get 10 clients? If you spend $300 and you get 10 clients, then $30 is your acquisition cost. If each one of those customers only spends $5 in your business, you have a net loss of $25 per person, which gives you a net loss of $250. So, the idea behind it is you must find out first what your acquisition cost is. Next, what is break-even cost, daily, weekly or monthly? Then ask yourself how you get customers to continue to buy from you. Think of this as "lifetime value." Now let's use the same equation – if you spend $300 on any type of marketing for two weeks, and you get 10 clients? If you spend $300 and you get 10 clients, then $30 is your acquisition cost. If each one of those customers only spends $5 in your business, you have a net loss of $25 per person, which gives you a net loss of $250 today. Suppose that customer is going to buy the same product each week for a year. That's a $30 acquisition cost; break-even is six weeks x $5 = $30. Your lifetime value first year is 40 weeks x $5 = $200. Now your ROI is 200/30 = 6.66x. You see now that everything must have an ROI.

The reality is that to do marketing well today, it's not like it used to be when you could hire one marketing person, and they could cover all the mediums required in today's world. You need to hire experts in each field. For example, if you're going to hire an expert in digital marketing, they need to be an expert in SEO and Google ads white papers. There needs to be an expert for LinkedIn, there needs to be an expert for YouTube, there needs to be an expert for Instagram, an expert for Twitter, and an expert for Facebook. There needs to be a marketing person who's an expert in buying media because you can't have a company that has a marketing person who can do all of it. It's a sad reality but true that if somebody is not focused on it 100% of the time, then really no one's doing it.

> **Action Item #12 – Figure out what your acquisition cost is per customer per marketing strategy.**

1% Changes Every Day

Finally, if we want incremental growth and delivery mastery, we must have systems and processes set up so that our products and services leave the building and go to our clients the same every time. Ask yourself: What systems and processes do you need to put into place to grow to the level that you see your business at? Itemize the daily tasks in your business that get repeated and see where you can delegate, outsource, or systemize so you free up space and time in your business. But let's not forget the people side of it. Whether you have five or 35 people in your business, you can still be a great leader. But in making incremental changes, every person you hire adds another level of complexity because you're not only managing additional different relationships. And when you have family members in the business, it's not just the dynamic with them. It's that as you're growing or changing to be where you need to go, how do these relationships change? How do these relationships with our children, sisters, brothers, and mother's cousins all start to shift? All this navigation takes skill, practice, and patience.

 **Key Takeaways**

➢ Figure out your debit ratio and what you need to do to pay debt at a faster rate;

➢ Do a task without delegating and you are destined to do it forever;

➢ Know your value and the values of your team;

➢ Surround yourself with trusted advisors;

➢ Figure out who you need to become for your business to grow;

➢ Marketing is always math; and

➢ Systemize the process so you can humanize the experience.

Chapter 6
Hiring is an Art Form

Hire character. Train skill.
—Peter Schulz

Hiring in today's market has changed. Back in my grandfather's or even my father's day, a business owner could say, "I need you to do this work for eight hours, and I need you to do as you're told." People would show up, do the work, and go home. But that's not how the world works anymore. Since the Covid-19 pandemic changed the entire notion of having to report to a physical office or cubicle farm five days a week, employers are now realizing that work can sometimes be done in different ways.

The world has changed in many ways in the past ten years, pandemics notwithstanding, yet the hiring process hasn't adapted to keep up with today's demands of an evolving workforce with different expectations than previous generations have had. Yet when you run a family business, you'll hire simply because you need a body. "Bobby's not doing anything today. Let me bring him in. He can do it." Don't get me wrong, that's how we did it in my family growing up. When I was younger, it was, "Hey, we're moving some people today. I got a truck to unload—you're coming to work with me." Back then the labor laws were: "If you're old enough to carry something, you're old enough to go to work," and my Dad and my Grandpa had that same belief. It didn't matter if you were only eight years old, you sucked it up. As hard as this sounds, it gave me a really good work ethic, and I wouldn't change my childhood for anything.

But hiring people just because they have a heartbeat and then wondering why they do everything wrong—whose fault is that? Short Answer is, YOU! You, as the business owner, by hiring your family members, forfeit the right to bitch about them because you're the one who's hired them. In fact, that goes to everybody you hire, not just family members. In business, we get the people we deserve. Maybe we don't deserve all the bad employees, but if you hire the wrong people, it'll be down to the person who made that call.

When I work with new businesses, the first thing I look for is their process for hiring, and I always ask clients these four questions:

- Did I teach the process to the people?
- Is the process correct?
- Are the people willing to follow the process?
- Where is the process?

Their answers will tell me how they approach hiring, where the gaps are, and where there is room for improvement. If they haven't taught the process to their team, that tells me they need simple processes to help delegate. If the person who creates the process can't articulate it to others, they themselves don't understand what the process is. Maybe the process is too complicated to teach or is even outdated. If they can't say if the process is correct, that tells me they don't use it or trust it, and we must figure out why that is. How have they been hiring up until that point? If their team isn't willing to follow the process, that's a big problem too. Why don't they follow it? What's getting in the way? And finally, where is this process kept? Is it in a manual that everyone can follow, or does it only exist in the business owner's heads?

In my business, we have a hiring process, and we use a recruitment manual to help guide the people doing the hiring. There aren't enough pages in this book to print this manual, and in it we keep our process for placing ads, advertising, callbacks, the phone interview process, in person interview process, decision making, and follow-ups. There's a pre-interview checklist, handouts, what we look for in a resume and more. This helps everyone to follow the same steps and make sure we get the best from our time. The process might adapt depending on the role you're advertising, but this way you're more likely to find success. When our applicants don't follow the process, send a resume to this email address or don't call in, it's a tell-tale sign that they will not follow the processes in our workplace.

When I work with clients, they're sometimes frustrated to learn that using a process slows everything down. (Slow down to speed up.) As a business owner, you're itching to hire someone new—"But I need a person now!" You'll get the people you deserve, remember? You don't want to rush this. HIRE SLOW, FIRE FAST. Plan and make sure you put aside the time and resources you'll need for hiring someone new. As a small or family-run business, you're well positioned to be flexible and adapt as needed. You want to weed people out and find the right person for your team, and you can only do that if you have systems to help you get there.

What I'm going to talk about in this chapter will go for everyone you hire—family and non-family members alike. Your sons or daughters might hate it, but the right to work for your company is still the right to work for your company, and they should expect to go through this process too. Just because you're related doesn't give them the right to do anything. We all follow the process no matter who anyone is.

Hiring For Attitude

Let's start with the position you're hiring for. People write job descriptions with too many words in them. Someone in that business who's super analytical has decided that everything about the role must be written out. But those job descriptions bore people. I'm not saying those words aren't important, but people just don't read the full job descriptions anymore. All it really boils down to is:

- What 4-6 OKRs/outcomes are they going to be responsible for? Daily, weekly, monthly, and yearly.

- What are the 8, 10, or 12 KAI/Standards/responsibilities for that role? Daily, weekly, monthly.

- And what 4-6 KBI behaviors do they need to have to do that? Hourly, daily, weekly, yearly.

Writing a job description with this in mind means you're letting people know what behaviors and attitudes you're looking for. You'll find people who are a better fit, and you'll waste less time sifting through mismatched candidates.

But it's not just ads you need to have a process for; you need to have a process for receiving those applications too. For example, if someone applies for an administrative assistant position, we ask them to provide their name, address, phone number and date of birth. We're doing this for two reasons. One: we're looking at it for a background check, and two: we're looking at it for a credit check. But depending on the position, I will also ask people to either handwrite the application or type it.

If it's an administrative assistant role, for example, I have them hand write the application because we, as the business, need to know their handwriting is legible—not like my chicken scratch writing. How is their spelling? What is their attention to detail? But this process will also help us look for those telltale signs about their attitude to work. Things like not taking the time to reprint the copy and rewrite it if they make a mistake. If they scribble the mistake out and write the new answer next to it. Details like this are important because some businesses won't have access to software that checks spelling and grammar. So, when they hire somebody in a role like this, they're looking for an executive administrative assistant they can trust who will take memos and notes correctly with no mistakes.

Hiring using a process that reveals candidate attitudes and behaviors is going to serve your business better in the long run. Stop making hiring decisions based on the skills you see on a resume. Skills can always be taught, and the skills you'll see on a resume will usually be an over-inflated version of what the person thinks they are. Meaning that anyone going through the interview process will either be a professional at mastering the interview process, or a professional at mastering their work. And you're going to get one or the other. Often, the one who gets through will be the one who is the better salesperson rather than the best person for the job. They'll be the one who can sell you on their over-inflated ego and their well-crafted resume. They'll be the ones saying, "I'm the best in the world, I have all these skills," but they won't tell you about their shitty attitude. If someone came to me and said, "You know, I'm not very good at this. But I'll work hard for you." I would probably give them a shot at an interview, because then I would have an idea of their attitude—their honesty and determination to improve.

Thinking About Psychographics

Another part of our process involves finding out about the potential candidate's psychographics. Anyone can ask: "Well,

Alex, tell me, how long have you been a manager?"

"Oh, I've been managing teams for the last 20 years," he might say. "I have these skills and those skills ..."

That's great, but it doesn't tell us anything about their personality, attitudes or beliefs. A list of skills on a resume doesn't reveal if their values and beliefs align with your business. Example questions are: How would they communicate a problem with the team? What motivates them to work, or lead?

In our process, the first thing we do is send them a list of pre-interview questions that help us to understand their psychographics. We don't ask anything about skill. Not one question asks them about their skills because we want to know what they have to say about themselves. We want to know what they're doing in life, what's driving them and what they value.

There are questions like, "What are the top three things you liked about your previous employer?" Or "What are the top three things you disliked?" We want people to answer questions that stir up their emotions because these answers will give us a true sign of who they really are. If they can't list two things they liked but can give you 35 things they didn't like, that tells you there was possibly a problem with the employer, not the candidate.

It's about bringing the real person back. "Tell me, what did you like about school? What didn't you like about school?" People might not be able to remember what they had for breakfast yesterday, but they will remember what they liked and disliked about middle school, and that will tell you something about them as a person. Change up the questions and ask them things about their life. We want to take people through a process that throws them off their game and throws out that salesperson. We must ask people questions they've never been asked before.

If they get through to the next stage, you can then use their answers to see if they were really paying attention and if the person you're getting is them or the salesperson. When you ask them, "If you joined our team, what would be your expectations?" You can see if their story matches with what they wrote. Will they be smart enough to say, "Well, what I put down was X," or will they list something completely different? It's making sure the stories match and that they are consistent throughout the process. If they aren't, that's a telltale sign that there could be problems in the future.

After the interview, we ask them to fill in a form and send it in. On this form, there are questions like:

- What did you hear this evening that touched you?
- What have you done in the past that you believe could add value to your story?
- What impossible hurdle have you overcome in your life that has caused you to believe you're a stayer?

That last question is important because right now, with the mass exodus of people leaving their jobs or re-evaluating their work-life harmony, it's important to find people who plan on staying. Asking these post-interview questions will help you find someone who will fit your company's culture and will reveal more about their attitude and values that might have been missed in the interview.

Hiring for attitude means I've heard everything, and it usually makes me laugh — "Hey, I'd love to work for you. But I need Wednesdays off. That's my golf day." They ask for Fridays off or come in and claim they ran their last company. You'll have people who say they were smarter than their colleagues, and now they're here to solve all the problems you have in your business, too. When you're bringing the real person back into the room, it can be very revealing. Weeding out the time-wasters and trouble-makers means you're more likely to find the right person for your business.

Group Interviews

If candidates make it through the phone interview, the written portion and the DISC assessment, we invite the top four or five to a group interview. We bring everyone into a room — or Zoom if necessary — and we do this because we want to watch for body language; 55% of everything someone says is in their body language, 38% is going to be in the inflection of their voice, and 7% is going to be in the words they use. In that group interview, you need to look for telltale signs that people will work well with others. Is their body language open or closed? Are they posturing, or are they meek and mild?

Let me give you an example of what a group interview was like in hiring a COO of a local non-profit. There will usually be three of us, myself and my clients. Sometimes, it might be just me and the business owner. We, the hiring team, are on one side of the room, and on the other side, you have the four or five top candidates. The interview process works like a round robin. We, the hiring team, all came up with a list of 10 questions each to ask during the group interview. Then, Hiring Team Member Number One on our side will ask Candidate Number Five on the opposite side a question. They'll answer the question, and then Hiring Team Member Number Two on our side will ask a different question to Candidate Number Four on the other side.

A true telltale sign to watch out for is if Number Four says, "No, no, I want to answer that question." I have to say, "I'm sorry, that's not how it works." When people get into a group interview, the gloves come off. We're looking for signs from people who want to control the conversation and want to be the alpha dog. By watching their behavior, you can see how good they will be at teamwork and collaborating as a team. When they communicate, do they take over the conversation or allow others time to speak?

At this stage, the ones who are the best at selling you on

their skills, who appear to have the best attitude, might have gotten through, but by doing our process, we take that power away from them. They can't prepare answers to questions ahead of time, and watching their body language will reveal a lot more about themselves than they will realize.

Ranking The Candidates

Once we run that entire process, we thank them and tell them what to expect over the coming days. Then, the next step for the hiring team is that nobody gets to talk. The business owner, the team, the family—there's no talking allowed. This step needs to be done without anybody else's input; it needs to stay logical and without emotion.

Here's what we do: everybody ranks each one of those people by how well they did by giving them a number. For example, for positivity we might give someone a six. But on neatness, maybe a zero because they came dressed in jeans with holes. Based on the answers to our interview questions, we rank them on common sense — do we think this person will be able to think on their feet, or would they just run when things get tough? Practical ability — can they function outside of rules? When you're looking for people who will join your team, you want to rank things like honesty and personal strength, as well as what your final impressions are.

Once we get through the numbers, then the hiring team can talk.

"So, how did Jane do?"

"OK, we gave her a 98. Tina scored 93. We gave Tim an 89."

The numbers don't lie, and by taking the emotion out of it, the hiring process is simpler and more efficient.

"Oh, Jane scored 95 on three of the four stages, and scored 98 on the fourth one."

"OK, that's the number one candidate. Let's put her in this bucket. Who's number two? Put them over here."

Doing it this way also means you can list off who you would not hire right away.

"This person's out because of X, Y and Z."

We talk through it as owners, we talk through it as a committee, and we drill down as to why this person would be a good fit. If everybody in the room is ranking a candidate by the numbers, the emotions don't get in the way.

As a hiring team, we agree—"yes" or "no," and everybody must sign off on it. The problems we see with interviews outside of our process go something like this:

"Tell me what you think of so-and-so?"

And you might say, "Oh my god, they looked nice. I like them. They just really resonated with me."

Well, if you have the same communication style as that person, that will be what did it for you. Not their attitude or potential to be a good employee. Taking the emotional part out of hiring means you can make it a logical process, and you're more likely to find the right fit.

Second Interview

Then we move on to the second interview, where you have those conversations about your business. Things like your minimum standards for working together, the rules everyone is expected to follow, and their potential responsibilities.

You are reminding people that they must earn the right to work with you, this isn't a carte blanche to do whatever they want. We recommend a 120-day to six-month probationary period, hitting standards every week, and you want the new employee to earn the right to keep their job. What that does for you as an organization is it allows you to really see the true colors of the people you hire. Everybody can be good for 90 days, but by putting in a probationary period that is unrealistic, you can stop the shenanigans and find out if the person you just hired really was right for your business.

When you end up with the wrong people, you think the problem is as simple as not finding "good people." That "people just don't want to work." I hate it when owners say that because I know it's not true—maybe they just don't want to work for you. A lot of people out there do want to work, but over the last few years they've found that their priorities have shifted, and they are less willing to put up with what doesn't work for them.

One of our friends works for a large corporation that has a processing facility with two thousand open positions.

"We have to fill them, but people just don't want to work," he sighed.

I shook my head. "Well, would you do that job for $18 an hour?"

"That's not the point—"

"Hell, yes, it's the point!"

You don't get to tell people what kind of work they're supposed to like or what industry they're supposed to enjoy. And if your business has that many positions open, it's not a hiring problem; it's a culture problem. I'll admit, I had to learn this lesson, too. I was one of those people who would say, "They just need to do what we say." But that's not enough. People want to know, "What's In It For Me?" They want purpose and meaning in their working day, and are no longer willing to work two or three jobs to get by.

People today are facing more challenges than we realize, and as we've all learned, with all the social and cultural issues going on in the world right now, there are many people stuck in a system that makes finding—and keeping— work, harder. There are people who are struggling to find hours in the day because they have to balance raising a family with finding daycare and work. People who are one flat tire away from losing their jobs. Let's be candid: poverty is $15 an hour, and there are people hiring at less than that wage. Is that job going to be worth their time? Is that job going to help them get out of poverty? Not everybody is trying to cheat the system and avoid work, but there are challenges that you, as the business owner, need to be aware of. By having a process that focuses on looking for people's attitudes over skills, you're going to find people who see your job opening as the answer to their needs.

In the next chapter, we will discuss systems, processes, and operations in your business.

Action Item #13 – Email us today andy@andyobrien.biz for your download of the Team Recruitment Manual.

 Key Takeaways

- People want to work, but they want to know WIIFM (What's In It For Me);
- You get the people you deserve;
- A hiring process looks for attitude and not skill; and
- Hiring should be logical, not emotional.

Chapter 7
A Primer on Operations

Building and scaling an impactful business
requires a drive beyond making money.
Having the passion to deliver on your company's
purpose will fuel you through the trying times.
—Ken Lin, Founder of Credit Karma

In a larger corporate entity or business, operations are divided into standard departments like the C-Suite, middle management, IT, or Human Resources. In a family-run business, operations fall under "whoever can do it best." To be fair, this may include information systems, technology, automation, workflow automation, standard operating procedures or SOPs. When it comes to a family business, this can be a huge problem in the organization, because often a family member who happens to be a good technician, or a really good auto mechanic, suddenly gets made the leader of the band.

But just because you're good at doing a particular job doesn't mean you are good at managing people. Toyota is an often-used example of being a master of operational effectiveness. They were the first to implement kaizen, which is the Japanese word for continuous improvement. In the context of business, it refers to activities that continuously improve all functions and all employees, from the top of the organization all the way down to the bottom.

The heart and soul of operations is setting up processes or standard operating procedures for every entity in the operation. We usually think about systems and processes when we look at quality control or delivery mastery. But one of the biggest failures of companies in quality control is that people try to circumvent the process. So, in building the process, we must make sure it's the right process for the result that we want. Then we need to ensure that people will follow the process. The last thing to consider is where does the process live? In every part of building a process, the quickest and easiest methodology is that if somebody is good at getting that thing done, then we want to make that replicable.

Again, first decide on your outcome, then work backwards into what steps take place next, all the way back to the beginning. Then we start the process of building systems. Let's take a moment and look at John Maxwell's Five Levels of Leadership and see how we can apply that to your organization.

Position

One of the caveats when building a system or a process is people end up falling into unconscious incompetence, which is one of the four levels of learning I'll touch on. For example, we don't know that we cannot do something – we don't know what we don't know. Take a toddler, for instance. Does a toddler know they can drive a car and the benefits of being able to? The answer is obviously no. They are unable to recognize the deficit. Now, a child who is slightly older, who has more experience and can understand the significance of the skills that they lack, is consciously incompetent.

The child is then a teenager, heading to drivers ed where they learn to check their mirrors and go through all the precautionary steps they are taught every time they get into the vehicle; this stage is called conscious competence. The teenager understands and has the knowledge to drive, but it takes concentration and heavy conscious involvement. The last stage is unconscious competence. The knowledge and skills have been fully attained and mastered to the point of second nature. You can lose track of time, and the task that once took intense conscious focus is now habitual. The principle about building processes where things get missed is that so many people who do the tasks have unconscious competence where, just like driving a car, it becomes habitual. What ends up happening is you're left with missing steps. As I said earlier, to build the process out, we need to start with the end in mind and work backwards in every department of the business, from IT to customer service. We must ensure the customer experience is exceptional.

People, process, product, profit – you get the right people, you teach them your process, they're not allowed to change the process until they've mastered the process, then you look at the product and service that you have. If your people are good, your process is solid, you have a good or great product, and you will always have profit. We are essentially building how-to manuals for every department of our business so that the next person who comes in can be trained on the exact same process.

E-Myth Process

In Michael Gerber's 1986 book entitled The E-Myth Revisited: Why Most Small Businesses Don't Work and What to Do About It, he touches on the process that the McDonald's brothers had built in 1954. A food assembly line derived from Henry Ford's (Ford Motors) first factory assembly line created in 1913, the brothers drew out every step of their process on a tennis court and had their workers practice the flow and who did what, when and how. Their process made it simple, so simple that even a teenager with zero work experience could jump right in and run the lines just as well as anyone else. This is all to say that process is key, but a big problem I see today is that lots of business owners think that what they do is very difficult, and nobody can replace it, so they end up doing it themselves. This creates a bottleneck within the organization. By creating a 'How to Manual' you are not held hostage if someone quits or if an employee gets promoted. You can continue to move people into your organization quickly and allow for scalability within your company.

Document It

The fear of losing control of a business, especially in a small business, is common. When dealing with this issue, we must sit down collectively as a group and work backwards. I worked with a family business on this subject – we had 13 people in the room, including three owners and executive staff. I was asking them questions regarding their shipping process. One owner said that everyone knows the process inside and out, but when I told each of the 13 people to write on a sticky note what their process was, I got 13 different answers. Everybody else thought they knew what the process was, and they kept doing it wrong. Because there wasn't clarity – the process wasn't written down anywhere for anyone to refer to. Do a task without documenting it, and you are destined to do it FOREVER! Simple process: Have the person who is doing the KAI key activity write down everything they are doing, NOW, while they are in the process.

Product Development

While we were working with some businesses through the Covid-19 pandemic, we saw that product development is not just a product but how we switch our model of business. One of the businesses we coached was a struggling dine-in-only restaurant. However, they decided to implement a drive-through into their business model. They had better months over the pandemic with just the drive-through than they ever did with people dining in. In product development, we are always looking and asking: what are we going to do next? Product development is niche. It is about finding that sliver of pie that nobody can duplicate.

I see it a lot with family businesses that when they are asked who their target market or ideal customer is, they reply with "anyone with a heartbeat or who can fog a mirror" because they just want to make money. What this means is that you think you can compete with the Walmart and Targets of the world. Why would you want to do that? You need to have a crystal clear target market and demographic you are trying to hit.

Cabin Coffee Company

When we talk about finding a niche in a market, the Cabin Coffee Company is a perfect example of a business that has succeeded and continues to succeed. Cabin Coffee Co. started in Clear Lake, Iowa, in 2002 but has since franchised out to 25 different locations across the United States. 2002 was a big year for a large coffee company like Starbucks, opening 250+ stores on top of their already large and growing franchise of 1,078 stores in continental North America. Seeing these numbers of a rapidly growing franchise that recently went public at the time may be off putting and intimidating for a small coffee company in Clear Lake, Iowa – IF their niche was to grow and focus less on quality over exponential growth. Cabin Coffee Company, however, focused on handmade food, not microwaved snacks. They have found a niche of quality, customer experience, atmosphere and family-owned flair while being able to franchise and expand their business.

Innovation and Bell Curve

Innovating is something that every single company needs to focus on in some capacity. Innovation steps through hardship and creates companies that may not have been created otherwise. During the COVID pandemic, we saw many family-owned businesses NOT changing their business models to mold with the times. (I know mindset and I've always done it this way.) Many waited around to see what other businesses around them were doing. The companies that got in real trouble are the ones that reacted after the fact. (Laggards.)

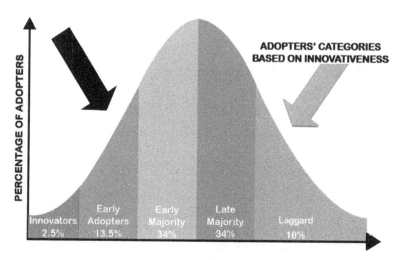

There are five types of adopters of innovation in the world of business: Innovators, Early Adaptors, Early Majority, Late Majority and Laggards. When we look at the bell curve of innovation, we see the graph broken up into five segments, with 'innovators' making up just 2.5% of the population and Early/Late Majority making up 34%, respectively. It's important, when we talk about businesses, to take risks in the niche that the business is focused in. Uber is a great example of innovation and risk taking. In 2010, Uber was released and completely changed the travel industry in major cities across the globe. Uber went into an industry that had been relatively unshaken for over a hundred years. In 1970, fully licensed taxicabs made 2.4 billion passenger trips in the United States. Uber created innovation in an untouched industry and created a process so simple that anyone with a valid license and a car could become a taxi driver. They are the gold standard for everything we have touched on in this chapter.

Action Item #14 – Do a SWOT analysis on each and every employee – Do you need a quick tutorial on how to do a SWOT of your people? Email us at <u>andy@andyobrien.biz</u>

 Key Takeaways

- ➢ Have a process to develop the organization;
- ➢ Don't hire a manager or leader based on their performance in a role. It's their performance with other people that counts;
- ➢ Write it down and put it in sight of everyone;
- ➢ Always look to the future of what's next (front side of the curve); and
- ➢ Hope for the best is not a model – plan for it.

Chapter 8
We're All Going to Die One Day: Legacy

If you're going to live, leave a legacy.
Make a mark on the world that can't be erased.
—Maya Angelou

John D. Rockefeller Sr. is often associated with being one of the wealthiest men in history while pushing philanthropic acts and charitable donations. He started his career as a 16-year-old bookkeeper with a dream of making $100,000 and living to the age of 100. From there he built an oil dynasty making what would now equate to $17 billion. However, the Rockefeller name has not always been synonymous with giving. Rockefeller was accused of crushing out competition and building his fortune on the ruins of other men. In 1901 Rockefeller Sr.'s only son, John D. Rockefeller Jr., with deep-rooted religious beliefs and interests in social progression and philanthropy, started the Institute for Medical Research, now named Rockefeller University, with the mission of 'Conducting science on behalf of humanity.' A year later he would start The General Board Of Education with the initiative to improve the education system in the south. John D. Rockefeller Jr. completely changed his family name and legacy.

If it weren't for Rockefeller Jr.'s new and different approach to doing business, the Rockefeller name may have been tarnished throughout history. It's these new and exciting ideas that come from the second and third generation family business owners that can be so pivotal, but a common problem we see in family-owned businesses is the first generation.

Owners expect their children to be able to run a business with no initial background or passion for the business to begin with; while holding back key information that may or may not put a good light on you as an owner, father, mother, uncle, aunt, grandpa or, etc.

Most family owners never plan the exit. This should be planned first when the business is started. As the title states, there are always two exits, and you are only in control of the planned one.

You need to give them a clear line of sight to what the vision, mission and goals of the business are, how you got to today and how you planned on getting to the future vision plan. Many family businesses are moved to generations based on the oldest child instead of who in the family has the passion, purpose and drive to carry the legacy on. This starts when they are growing up, sweeping floors, carrying lampshades, working on the line, in customer service and answering to someone other than you. The principle behind it is giving them clarity as they move up the ladder, so that later on they are able to have a full understanding of the business, of all of its departments, and how it runs from the inside to the outside.

Too often, legacy is based on vanity. There are two ways vanity gets in the way of legacy. One way is by being too focused on who will carry your name forward rather than on how the company can sustain itself through generations by keeping up with changing times. For example, as a family, you can discuss and decide on the future potential of preparing the business to be sold if it becomes too much to maintain and perhaps the next generation does not want to carry it forward. This causes major friction in the business. Why? you ask. Because the patriarch or matriarch of the family has put their blood, sweat and tears into something they believe is bigger than any of the offspring, and they can't believe, or refuse to believe, no one would want to carry this forward. I've seen it first hand three times, and it always ends badly for the relationship and the wills being rewritten out of spite for the children. NOW, don't get me wrong, some of these spoiled rotten family members are also assholes, so write them out of the will.

The second way is about the value of your "name." In some cases where businesses have been around for 30 to 40 years, the name has buyer recognition, buyer staying power or customer experience (this drives the value up). Some other business comes with owners feeling that who will carry on the name is more important than how the business will carry on and make money. Remember earlier I stated in marketing that only you and your mother want to see your name on a billboard, sign or in lights..

In our experience, a portion of a family-owned business should have to pay fair market value (yes, I said it: PAY FOR THE BUSINESS). This can create difficult conversations with regard to what the second generation receives.

Let's say someone wants to be a part owner in their family business, and they also have kids – college tuition and mortgages to consider. They don't have coffers of money waiting for them. There are a few different ways to look at a situation like this. This is more **complicated** than this analogy and will take a professional mergers and acquisition broker, a lawyer, and your accountant, but here's the idea: First and foremost, you could structure a deal that would allow them to create wealth/ownership in the business by deferring any pay increases year over year and then the profits they may receive year to year can also be deferred into shares of the business. Over the course of ten years, if the ratio is one to one, he or she will be able to own a 15% stake in the business when it comes time for them to buy the organization. This also opens up the opportunity to be able to go to the bank, get a loan and leverage oneself and its existing shares to be able to buy more shares of the business. Again, this is gorilla math, and it will take several professionals to help organize this structure.

Now, for all you kids or siblings reading this, you will not have a complete say, and just because you own shares doesn't mean you don't have to do your job EVERY day any longer. You are still an employee until board meetings. Nothing ruins culture in a company than when this goes sideways with positional power and the newly bought shares drive your/their ego into the stratosphere, and don't tell me you weren't warned. This will drive a wedge between you, the owners, and the team.

Now, many of you are squeamish about the word divorce. Heck, you should have planned and written the divorce decree/the break up plan (think of it like a prenuptial) before you bring family member partners into the business. It's a document that lists all the things that can happen, go wrong, or you may disagree about in the business and an agreement that if X happens, then you will agree to do Y. You will also have a document that will list out your operating agreement, your governance and voting rights as family members. Now again, some of you are saying to yourself, "This won't happen to us," or "What a waste of time." I've witnessed it first hand, and the cliché "shit happens," is real. Racism, bigotry, infidelity, ignorance and arrogance are just a few of the reasons to write these documents up. Now think of that friend or colleague who went through a divorce – do you recall how much fun they had dividing up their personal effects and kids? Now add the complexity of owning a business with employees and the trickle-down effect this has on your business and its customers. DRAMA is now your Karma for a poor plan.

As I mentioned earlier, to create a legacy, every business should have a buy-sell agreement in place. A buy and sell agreement (or buy-sell agreement) is a legally binding contract that stipulates how a partner's share of a business may be reassigned if that partner dies or otherwise leaves the business. Most often, the buy and sell agreement stipulates that the available share be sold to the remaining partners or the partnership. Buy-sell agreements often use life insurance policies to fund the potential buyout in the event of a partner's death.

A buy and sell agreement may also be called a buyout agreement, a business will, or a business prenup. Buy-sell agreements are between all owners. When you buy a key person insurance policy – this is when the business takes the life insurance policy out on key personnel or shareholders to protect the business in case this person is hurt or dies prematurely. If that person is paid $150,000 a year and they own $700,000 in shares, this allows the business to have a life insurance policy for a million dollars on said employee, as an example. The most important thing for the business is its ability to buy the shares of that person from their family, which gives the family X amount of cash to live on, also known as a buy-sell agreement.

The second thing that it does is it allows you to be able to afford to pay somebody to come in and take the position of a recently deceased member of the business. That $150,000 allows for hiring a president or a CEO of the business to help it run in the first year and provides cash to move the business forward. This is all extremely crucial for a family-owned business to have in place. When we talk about legacy, it's important to understand how to create longevity and passion for the business from generation to generation. Roughly 30% of family-owned businesses make it to the second generation, only 12% to the third, and a minuscule 3% make it to the fourth generation.

Another aspect of creating longevity and legacy is through transparency and trust within the business. We had a client who had passed away. He was in the process of gathering data to share with his family at the time. Unfortunately, he never shared any critical information with anyone; none of his employees or family knew how to run the business. He was not only the chief cook and bottle washer, but the CEO, CFO, Chief salesperson and chief manager of AR and AP, so no one knew where any of that vital information was kept. So, in this case, there was no influx of cash to hire someone of that caliber to take control of the business. It all comes back to not having Key Person Insurance.

> **Action Item #15** – Find all of these documents in your business, NOW! Review them and determine if they need to be refreshed or rewritten. If you don't have a buy-sell agreement or a Key Person Policy on anyone. Email us at andy@andyobrien.biz

Now let's say they want to sell the business, and you believe the business is worth $1 million (no valuation); because all the vital information of the business is hidden and not written down in a manual, that business is worth 40% less than the market value and no one, I mean no one wants to buy you and keep you in the business long-term. Most owners after the sale will fight tooth and nail every time the new owner wants to make changes, has ideas or wants to hire new people.

We will take you through a business growth process. It's the process of setting up the business so that it runs without you in it every day. Then the business is run by someone other than you, and maybe you're buying and running a second business. As I have mentioned throughout the book, every good business owner needs an accountant, an attorney, a business coach, and a banker because when we start talking about legacy and how the business is going to be set up, we want to talk to experts in those fields. We want to create exit-ability and wealth events in the business. We have partners that we use specifically to help write plans for the business owners so that the business can give the next of kin a way to buy the business in the end and allow them a way to find professionals who will do that. Such as an attorney, they're going to allow them to set it up legally and minimize any fighting for the business if something does happen. Along with an attorney, an accountant is vital to any small business that wants to succeed and create a legacy.

When everybody's surprised at the reading of the will, there is a problem. I don't care what business you're in, if you leave all that shit to chance, and you leave it for the executor of the estate between siblings to talk about who does what, where, and when, it'll end up being a shit show. It just will. That's how it plays out. Because somebody somewhere thinks they deserve more than the other person, that then leads to a whole other set of problems. So, part of building a legacy is ensuring you have your systems and processes in place. Once you write them down, what you and your spouse or significant other want to do, that's when you start having the conversations, and you start grooming the people around you to do those roles. Because at the end of the day, you do not want surprises.

One of the greatest pieces of advice that I was ever given by a client who works in the automotive world is when he said to me, "Because I have four children with different personalities, they all must go and work for somebody for a minimum of five years... before they come and work for me. I need them to learn what it's like to listen. I need them to learn what it's like to follow instructions. I need them to learn what it's like out there, away from mom and dad, so that when they enter our organization, there's not so much disruption." He's moving them through with limited amounts of disruption in the business because of their newfound ability to go work for somebody else.

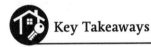 **Key Takeaways**

- ➢ Have a buy-sell agreement;
- ➢ Have key person life insurance;
- ➢ Write down everything in your business; and
- ➢ Always look to the legacy of what's next for the business and the people you are bringing along with you.

Chapter 9
It's time to F.I.T.F.O.

So many family business owners walk around like
a glow stick until someone, like me slaps them and
shakes them until the light comes on.
—Andy O'Brien

Family businesses aren't any harder or easier than any other business; the only difference is that you and your family make everything personal. Yes, I'm talking to you.

It's time to put all that emotion aside and F.I.T.F.O. (Figure it the fuck out) your business. You must start planning today. Where do you want this business to be in 1, 3, 5, 10, 12 or 20 years? How much, revenue, PROFIT, dividends, hours that you work, your role, value of the business, multiple earnings of valuation, and most of all, when are you done working in the business. These are the easy questions. You will NOT have all the answers today, and someday is tomorrow. If it's never documented, you will always wonder, struggle, and, most of all, live to work every day. No one (let me repeat), not one of your family or employees, is a mind reader. You need to start planning for success every 90 days. You need to STOP having super-hero-itis (I can do it better and faster than taking the time to train anyone) and allow your family and employees to grow with you in the day to day operations of the business.

You need to find a trusted advisor who will be collaborative and help guide you to the next level. Who won't take any of your shit, whining and "I know" mindset. Yes, all us owners have egos and think, "No one knows my business like I do." You're right and wrong. All the time, I hear, "My business is different and runs differently than XYZ." I call bullshit. Your business runs on the same chassis as all other businesses. YOU must learn from the business lessons in this book. You must take action every day.

In this short book, I lay out 15 specific action items that, on a micro level, will help immediately. Try it, one action item a week, and you have just 15x your learnings and your systems and processes with information you can use to grow your business. I also put together at the end of each chapter all the takeaways you will need to process to move your FAMILY forward in business.

Knowledge is not power – application of knowledge is powerful. DO something now – don't wait. SO many people (97%) just like you buy books, read a few chapters and then do nothing with the information. Be one of the 3% that take action, write goals down and move their family to the next level. Maybe it's your first vacation, a raise, a new car, or a new P.O.S. system for your business. I don't care; just do something. The goal of this book has been to help you improve your productivity, profitability, and achieve your long-term goals and vision for the business while keeping your most important relationships intact. Don't be too hard on yourself as you try to break old habits and learn new ones.

In this book, we have just scratched the surface of strategies and tactics that have worked with many family businesses. I hope you have found it a useful journey and resource to check back in with as you work to improve your systems and the functioning of your own business. I am a Son of a boss (S.O.B.). I wrote this book to spare you the pain of disappointment or discouragement in yourself, your family and the business. I've lived many of these mistakes (I have the teeshirt and the wounds to prove it), and I have guided hundreds of wives, husbands, daughters, sons, grandparents, aunts and uncles just like you through these wild waters of life and the Family Business business.

If you can't or won't do this for yourself and you're looking for that trusted advisor, coach, mentor and teacher, call or email me today <u>andy@andyobrien.biz</u> for your free expert business strategy session.

Endnotes

1. Brad Sugars ActionCOACH founder and CEO.

2. https://www.forbes.com/sites/nextavenue/2017/03/08/how-family-businesses-can-set-workfamily-boundaries/?sh=1bd6 2d3c2a80.

3. https://en.wikipedia.org/wiki/Parkinson%27s_law.

4. Jenyns, David, Systemology: Create Time, Reduce Errors, and Scale Your Profits with Proven Business Systems, SYSTEMology, 2020.

5. Credit: John Maxwell.

Action Items

Action Item #1 – If you're struggling with any of these issues in your business, here is a gift that keeps giving! Email us at andy@andyobrien.biz to get your complimentary questionnaire to show you where you need guidance and collaboration in your business.

Action Item #2 – You want to know if your family is in alignment in the business? Email us at andy@andyobrien.biz for your Expert complimentary strategy alignment session.

Action Item #3 – Do you want to learn more about yourself and your management and leadership abilities? Take a 360 assessment and learn what others in your business think about you. Email andy@andyobrien.biz for your assessment.

Action Item #4 – Go back to the above chart and add your numbers into the equation. Which of the numbers do you actually track today? Call me today for your seven-ways yearly spreadsheet download.

Action Item #5 – What is your debt-to-credit ratio? Current assets/Current liabilities = The amount of liquid assets available to liquidate current debt to the company's ability to meet current obligations.

Action Item # 6 – Run a quick cash flow analysis.

Action Item #7 – Want to create a budget based on the next three months? Email us at andy@andyobrien.biz for the free download of your yearly budget.

Action Item #8 – If you are the owner, CEO, president, etc., SPEAK LAST and not until everyone has expressed their ideas, strategies, tactics or opinions.

Action Item #9 – Call your accountant and take them to lunch. Ask them all the questions you're afraid to ask or afraid of the answer to! The only dumb questions in business today are the ones you don't ask.

Action Item #10 – Figure out what your time is worth to the business based on a 40-hour work week and two weeks vacation. For all of you saying I work more than that all the time... Maybe you're part of the problem.

Action Item #11 – What is your average dollar sale? Yes, all of your sales divided by the total tickets. Invoices or customer count.

Action Item #12 – Figure out what your acquisition cost is per customer per marketing strategy.

Action Item #13 – Email us today andy@andyobrien.biz for your download of the Team Recruitment Manual.

Action Item #14 – Do a SWOT analysis on each and every employee – Do you need a quick tutorial on how to do a SWOT of your people? Email us at andy@andyobrien.biz

Action Item #15 – Find all of these documents in your business, NOW! Review them and determine if they need to be refreshed or rewritten. If you don't have a buy-sell agreement or a Key Person Policy on anyone. Email us at andy@andyobrien.biz

Key Takeaways

Chapter 1

- Work to separate business and family;
- Find ways to create boundaries;
- Define clear and concise roles; and
- Know when to walk away – just because they're family, are they a good fit for the organization?

Chapter 2

- Don't be reactive in business, always look for solutions;
- Picking your partners and proper buy-sell agreements save time, energy and a shit ton of money;
- Don't hire your friends;
- Don't try to screw the government at the expense of your people;
- Raising your price is an emotional fear, not a reality;
- Figure out where you can maximize your profitability;
- Understand the difference between working *on* or *in* the business – set up systems; and
- Play to your strengths, hire to your weaknesses.

Chapter 3

- You must be a great follower first; then and only then can you lead;
- Teach first, then HIT them with the fish; Hire Coaching, FFS to figure it out;
- Understand that not one of you is as smart as all your people combined; and
- Keep your personal shit out of the business.

Chapter 4

- Know your numbers;
- If you don't measure your numbers, you can't fix, adapt or grow them;
- If you don't learn, learn, learn about profit, you will not have any; and
- Profit must be built into all aspects of your business, including your time.

Chapter 5

- Figure out your debit ratio and what you need to do to pay debt at a faster rate;
- Do a task without delegating and you are destined to do it forever;
- Know your value and the values of your team;
- Surround yourself with trusted advisors;
- Figure out who you need to become for your business to grow;
- Marketing is always math; and

> Systemize the process so you can humanize the experience.

Chapter 6

> People want to work, but they want to know WIIFM (What's In It For Me);
> You get the people you deserve;
> A hiring process looks for attitude and not skill; and
> Hiring should be logical, not emotional.

Chapter 7

> Have a process to develop the organization;
> Don't hire a manager or leader based on their performance in a role. It's their performance with other people that counts;
> Write it down and put it in sight of everyone;
> Always look to the future of what's next (front side of the curve); and
> Hope for the best is not a model – plan for it.

Chapter 8

> Have a buy-sell agreement;
> Have key person and life insurance;
> Write down everything in your business; and
> Always look to the legacy of what's next for the business and the people you are bringing along with you.

About Atmosphere Press

Founded in 2015, Atmosphere Press was built on the principles of Honesty, Transparency, Professionalism, Kindness, and Making Your Book Awesome. As an ethical and author-friendly hybrid press, we stay true to that founding mission today.

If you're a reader, enter our giveaway for a free book here:

SCAN TO ENTER
BOOK GIVEAWAY

If you're a writer, submit your manuscript for consideration here:

SCAN TO SUBMIT
MANUSCRIPT

And always feel free to visit Atmosphere Press and our authors online at atmospherepress.com. See you there soon!

Who is Andy O'Brien?

ANDY O'BRIEN has an energy that is infectious. His unique way of connecting life and business is something that benefits anyone attending his presentations. As one of the top coaches in the world, Andy O'Brien brings over twenty-five years of exceptional leadership and personal development experience to executives and business owners. In addition to coaching executives & business owners, he conducts public & private workshops & seminars. He is an inspirational keynote speaker, a results-oriented business coach and a global trainer for coaches around the world.

Working with Andy O'Brien ensures that your business is taken to the next level with increased efficiency, productivity and profitability. Through his unique approach to coaching and development, he can help you reach those goals – no matter how big or small.

Trust Andy O'Brien to equip you with the correct knowledge and skillset for long-term success – contact him today! Don't delay - be water, be powerful, and be successful!

www.AndyOBrien.Biz
https://www.linkedin.com/in/coachactionandy/
https://www.instagram.com/andyobrienatx/
https://www.facebook.com/andrew.obrien.1650
https://www.youtube.com/@UnfilteredNakedTruth
https://actioncoachcentraltx.com

Printed in the USA
CPSIA information can be obtained
at www.ICGtesting.com
LVHW090154150224
771924LV00005B/73